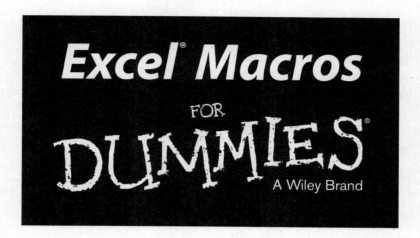

Excel® Macros

FOR DUMMIES®

A Wiley Brand

by Michael Alexander

FOR DUMMIES®
A Wiley Brand

Contents at a Glance

Table of Contents

Part III: One-Touch Data Manipulation 113

Chapter 6: Feeling at Home on the Range 115

Introduction

In its broadest sense, a *macro* is a sequence of instructions that automates some aspect of Excel so that you can work more efficiently and with fewer errors. You might create a macro, for example, to format and print a month-end sales report. After you develop the macro, you can execute it to perform many time-consuming procedures automatically.

Macros are written in VBA, which stands for Visual Basic for Applications. VBA is a programming language developed by Microsoft and a tool used to develop programs that control Excel.

Excel programming terminology can be a bit confusing. For example, VBA is a programming language but also serves as a macro language. What do you call something written in VBA and executed in Excel? Is it a macro or is it a program? Excel's Help system often refers to VBA procedures as *macros*, so this is the terminology used in this book.

You'll also see the term *automate* throughout this book. This word means that a series of steps are completed automatically. For example, if you write a macro that adds color to some cells, prints the worksheet, and then removes the color, you have automated those three steps.

You're probably aware that people use Excel for thousands of different tasks. Here are just a few examples:

- Keeping lists of things, such as customer names and transactions
- Budgeting and forecasting
- Analyzing scientific data
- Creating invoices and other forms
- Developing charts from data

The list could go on and on. The point is simply that Excel is used for a wide variety of tasks, and everyone reading this book has different needs and expectations regarding Excel. One thing most readers have in common, however, is the need to automate some aspect of Excel, which is what macros (and this book) are all about.

About This Book

This book approaches the topic of Excel macros with the recognition that programming VBA takes time and practice — time that you may not have right now. In fact, many analysts don't have the luxury of taking a few weeks to become expert at VBA. So instead of the same general overview of VBA topics, this book provides some of the most commonly used real-world Excel macros.

Each section in the book outlines a common problem and provides an Excel macro to solve the problem — along with a detailed explanation of how the macro works and where to use it.

Each section presents the following:

- The problem
- The macro solution
- How the macro works

After reading each section, you'll be able to

- Immediately implement the required Excel macro
- Understand how the macro works
- Reuse the macro in other workbooks or with other macros

The macros in this book are designed to get you up and running with VBA in the quickest way possible. Each macro tackles a common task that benefits from automation. The idea here is to learn through application. This book is designed so that you can implement the macro while getting a clear understanding of what the macro does and how it works.

Foolish Assumptions

I make three assumptions about you as the reader:

- You've installed Microsoft Excel 2007 or a higher version.
- You have some familiarity with the basic concepts of data analysis, such as working with tables, aggregating data, creating formulas, referencing cells, filtering, and sorting.
- You have an Internet connection so you can download the sample files.

Icons Used In This Book

Throughout this book, you'll see a few nifty icons that call out items that deserve special mention. Here is a list of these icons and what they mean.

Technical icons outline some of the technical aspects of the topic being discussed.

Tip icons cover tricks or techniques related to the current discussion.

Remember icons indicate notes or asides that are important to keep in mind.

Warning icons hold critical information about pitfalls you will want to avoid.

Beyond the Book

In additional to the material in the print or ebook you're reading, this product comes with more online goodies:

✔ **Sample files:** Each macro in this book has an associated sample file that enables you to see the macro working and to review the code. You can use the sample files also to copy and paste the code into your environment (as opposed to typing each macro from scratch). Download the sample files at

`www.dummies.com/extras/excelmacros`

Each macro in this book has detailed instructions on where to copy and paste the code. In general terms, you open the sample file associated with the macro, go to Visual Basic Editor (by pressing Alt+F11), and copy the code. Then you go to your workbook, open Visual Basic Editor, and paste the code in the appropriate location.

Note that in some macros, you need to change the macro to suit your situation. For instance, in the macro that prints all workbooks in a directory (see Chapter 4), you point to the C:\Temp\ directory. Before using this macro, you must edit it to point to your target directory.

If a macro is not working for you, most likely a component of the macro needs to be changed. Pay special attention to range addresses, directory names, and any other hard-coded names.

✔ **Cheat sheet:** The cheat sheet offers shortcut keys that can help you work more efficiently in Excel's Visual Basic Editor. You can find the cheat sheet at

www.dummies.com/cheatsheet/excelmacros

✔ **Web extras:** You'll find some great references that you can use, including a resume template, a sample resume, and a list of websites of value to networking professionals. Go to

www.dummies.com/extras/excelmacros

✔ **Updates:** If we have any updates to this book, you can find them at

www.dummies.com/go/excelmacroupdates

Where to Go from Here

If you're new to Excel macros, start with Chapters 1–3 to get the fundamentals you'll need to leverage the macros in this book. You'll gain a concise understanding of how macros and VBA work, along with the basic foundation you'll need to implement the macros provided in this book

If you have some macro experience and want to dive right into the macro examples, feel free to peruse Chapters 4–9 for a task or macro that looks interesting to you. Each macro example stands on its own; within each section, you get all the guidance you'll need to understand and implement the code in your own workbook.

Visit Chapters 4 and 5 if you're interested in macros that automate common workbook and worksheet tasks to save time and gain efficiencies.

Explore Chapters 6 and 7 to find macros that navigate ranges, format cells, and manipulate the data in your workbooks.

If you want to find macros that automate redundant pivot table and chart tasks as well as macros that send emails and attachments, thumb through the macros in Chapters 8 and 9.

Don't forget to read Chapters 10 and 11 for some useful tips and advice on how to get the most out of your new macro skills.

Here are some final things to keep in mind while working with the macros in this book:

- ✔ **Any file that contains a macro must have the .xlsm file extension.** See the section on macro-enabled file extensions in Chapter 1 for more information.

- ✔ **Excel will not run macros until they are enabled.** As you implement these macros, you and your customers must comply with Excel's macro security measures. See the section in Chapter 1 on macro security in Excel for details.

- ✔ **You cannot undo macro actions.** When working in Excel, you can often undo the actions you've taken because Excel keeps a log (called the undo stack) recording your last 100 actions. However, running a macro automatically destroys the undo stack, so you can't undo the actions you take in a macro.

- ✔ **You need to tweak the macros to fit your workbook.** Many of the macros reference example sheet names and ranges that you may not have in your workbook. Be sure to replace references such as Sheet 1 or Range("A1") with the sheet names and cell addresses you are working with in your own workbooks.

Part I
Holy Macro Batman!

getting started
with

Excel Macros

In this part . . .

- ✔ Build a foundation for your macro skills with fundamental macro recording concepts.

- ✔ Get a solid understanding of the ground rules for using and distributing macros in Excel.

- ✔ Explore Excel's coding environment with a deep-dive of Visual Basic Editor.

- ✔ Explore how to leverage the Excel object model to start writing your own macros from scratch.

- ✔ Understand the roles played by variables, events and error handling in macro development.

Chapter 1

Macro Fundamentals

A macro is essentially a set of instructions or code that you create to tell Excel to execute any number of actions. In Excel, macros can be written or recorded. The key word here is *recorded*.

Recording a macro is like programming a phone number into your cell phone. On your phone, you first manually dial and save the number. Later, you can redial those numbers with the touch of a button. In Excel, you start recording a macro, and then you perform your intended actions. While you record, Excel gets busy in the background, translating your keystrokes and mouse clicks to a macro. This written code is known as Visual Basic for Applications (VBA). After the macro is recorded, you can play back those actions anytime you want.

In this chapter, you explore macros and learn how you can use them to automate recurring processes to simplify your life.

Why Use a Macro?

The first step in using macros is admitting you have a problem. Actually, you may have several problems:

> ✔ **Repetitive tasks:** As each new month rolls around, you have to crank out those reports. You have to import that data. You have to update those pivot tables. You have to delete those columns, and so on. Wouldn't it be nice if you could fire up a macro and have the more redundant parts of your reporting processes performed automatically?

✔ **Mistakes:** When you're repeatedly applying formulas, sorting, and moving things around manually, you're bound to make mistakes. Add looming deadlines and constant change requests, and your error rate goes up. Why not calmly record a macro, ensure that everything is running correctly, and then forget it? The macro will perform every action the same way every time you run it; reducing the chance of errors.

✔ **Awkward navigation:** Make your reports more user friendly, and those who have a limited knowledge of Excel, will appreciate your efforts. Macros can be used to dynamically format and print worksheets, navigate to specific sheets in your workbook, or even save the open document in a specified location. Your audience will appreciate these touches that help make perusal of your workbooks a bit more pleasant.

Macro Recording Basics

To start recording your first macro, you need to find Macro Recorder, which is on the Developer tab. Unfortunately, Excel comes out of the box with the Developer tab hidden — you may not see it on your version of Excel at first. If you plan to work with VBA macros, you'll want to make sure that the Developer tab is visible. To display this tab:

1. **Choose File⇨Excel Options.**

2. **In the Excel Options dialog box, select Customize Ribbon.**

3. **In the list box on the right, click to place a check mark next to Developer.**

4. **Click OK to return to Excel.**

Now that the Developer tab appears in the Excel ribbon, you can start Macro Recorder. Select Record Macro from the Developer tab. The Record Macro dialog box appears, as shown in Figure 1-1.

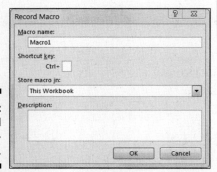

Figure 1-1:
The Record
Macro dia-
log box.

Here are the four parts of the Record Macro dialog box:

- ✔ **Macro name:** Excel gives a default name to your macro, such as Macro1, but you should give your macro a name more descriptive of what it does. For example, you might name a macro that formats a generic table FormatTable.

- ✔ **Shortcut key:** Every macro needs an event, or something to happen, for it to run. This event can be a button press, a workbook opening, or in this example, a keystroke combination. When you assign a shortcut key to your macro, entering that of keys triggers your macro to run. Note that you don't need a shortcut key to trigger a macro, so this field is optional.

- ✔ **Store macro in:** The This Workbook option is the default. Storing your macro in This Workbook simply means that the macro is stored along with the active Excel file. The next time you open that particular workbook, the macro is available to run. Similarly, if you send the workbook to another user, that user can run the macro as well (provided the macro security is properly set by your user — more on this later in this chapter).

- ✔ **Description:** This optional field can come in handy if you have numerous macros in a spreadsheet or you need to give a user a more detailed description about what the macro does.

With the Record Macro dialog box open, follow these steps to create a simple macro that enters your name in a worksheet cell:

1. **In the User Name field, enter a new single-word name for the macro to replace the default Macro1 name.**

   A good name for this example is MyName.

2. **In the Shortcut Key field, enter an uppercase N.**

   You've just assigned this macro to the shortcut key Ctrl+Shift+N.

3. **Click OK to close the Record Macro dialog box and begin recording your actions.**

4. **Select a cell in your Excel spreadsheet, type your name in the selected cell, and then press Enter.**

5. **Choose Developer⇨Code⇨Stop Recording (or click the Stop Recording button in the status bar).**

Examining the macro

The macro was recorded in a new module named Module1. To view the code in this module, you must activate Visual Basic (VB) Editor. You can activate VB Editor in either of two ways:

✔ Press Alt+F11.

✔ Choose Developer➪Code➪Visual Basic.

In VB Editor, the project window displays a list of all open workbooks and add-ins. This list is displayed as a tree diagram, which you can expand or collapse. The code that you recorded previously is stored in Module1 in the current workbook. When you double-click Module1, the code in the module appears in the Code window.

The macro should look something like this:

```
Sub MyName()
'
'  MyName Macro
'
'  Keyboard Shortcut: Ctrl+Shift+N
'
    ActiveCell.FormulaR1C1 = "Michael Alexander"

End Sub
```

The recorded macro is a Sub procedure named MyName. The statements tell Excel what to do when the macro is executed.

At the top of the procedure, note that Excel inserted some comments, which consist of information from the Record Macro dialog box. These comment lines (which begin with an apostrophe) aren't necessary, and deleting them has no effect on how the macro runs. If you ignore the comments, you'll see that this procedure has only one VBA statement:

```
ActiveCell.FormulaR1C1 = "Michael Alexander"
```

This single statement inserts in the active cell the name you typed while recording.

Placing a single apostrophe in front of any text of creates a *comment* and is called *commenting a line*. Commented lines will turn green and Excel will skip these lines when running the macro. Comments allow you to add your own notes in the code, giving you a chance to document what the code is doing, any business rules you've applied, or any other information you feel would help when reading the code.

Testing the macro

Before you recorded this macro, you set an option that assigned the macro to the Ctrl+Shift+N shortcut key combination. To test the macro, return to Excel by using either of the following methods:

✔ Press Alt+F11.

✔ Click the View Microsoft Excel button on the VB Editor toolbar.

When Excel is active, activate a worksheet. (It can be in the workbook that contains the VBA module or in any other workbook.) Select a cell and press Ctrl+Shift+N. The macro immediately enters your name into the cell.

In the preceding example, note that you selected the cell to be formatted before you started recording your macro. This step is important. If you select a cell while the macro recorder is turned on, that cell will be recorded into the macro. In such a case, the macro would always format that particular cell, and it would not be a general-purpose macro.

Editing the macro

After you record a macro, you can make changes to it (although you must know what you're doing). For example, assume that you want your name to be bold. You could re-record the macro, but editing the code is more efficient because this modification is simple. Press Alt+F11 to activate the VB Editor window. Then double-click Module1 and insert the following statement before the End Sub statement:

```
ActiveCell.Font.Bold = True
```

The edited macro appears as follows:

```
Sub MyName()
'
' MyName Macro
'
' Keyboard Shortcut: Ctrl+Shift+N
'
    ActiveCell.Font.Bold = True

    ActiveCell.FormulaR1C1 = "Michael Alexander"

End Sub
```

Test this new macro, and you see that it performs as it should.

Comparing Absolute and Relative Macro Recording

Now that you've read about the basics of the Macro Recorder interface, it's time to go deeper and begin recording macros. The first thing you need to understand before you begin is that Excel has two modes for recording: absolute reference and relative reference.

Recording macros with absolute references

Excel's default recording mode is absolute reference. When a cell reference in a formula is an *absolute reference,* it does not automatically adjust when the formula is pasted to a new location.

The best way to understand how this concept applies to macros is to try it out. Open the Chapter 1 Sample File.xlsx file and record a macro that counts the rows in the Branchlist worksheet. (See Figure 1-2.)

	A	B	C	D	E	F	G	H	I
1		Region	Market	Branch			Region	Market	Branch
2		NORTH	BUFFALO	601419			SOUTH	CHARLOTTE	173901
3		NORTH	BUFFALO	701407			SOUTH	CHARLOTTE	301301
4		NORTH	BUFFALO	802202			SOUTH	CHARLOTTE	302301
5		NORTH	CANADA	910181			SOUTH	CHARLOTTE	601306
6		NORTH	CANADA	920681			SOUTH	DALLAS	202600
7		NORTH	MICHIGAN	101419			SOUTH	DALLAS	490260
8		NORTH	MICHIGAN	501405			SOUTH	DALLAS	490360
9		NORTH	MICHIGAN	503405			SOUTH	DALLAS	490460
10		NORTH	MICHIGAN	590140			SOUTH	FLORIDA	301316
11		NORTH	NEWYORK	801211			SOUTH	FLORIDA	701309
12		NORTH	NEWYORK	802211			SOUTH	FLORIDA	702309
13		NORTH	NEWYORK	804211			SOUTH	NEWORLEANS	601310
14		NORTH	NEWYORK	805211			SOUTH	NEWORLEANS	602310
15		NORTH	NEWYORK	806211			SOUTH	NEWORLEANS	801607

Figure 1-2: Your pretotaled worksheet containing two tables.

You can find the sample data set used in this chapter on this book's companion website at www.dummies.com/extras/excelmacros. See this book's Introduction for more on the companion website.

Follow these steps to record the macro:

1. **Make sure cell A1 is selected.**

2. **On the Developer tab, select Record Macro.**

3. **Name the macro** AddTotal.

4. **Choose This Workbook for the save location.**

5. **Click OK to start recording.**

   At this point, Excel is recording your actions.

6. **While Excel is recording, select cell A16 and type** Total **in the cell.**

7. **Select the first empty cell in Column D (D16) and type** = COUNTA(D2:D15).

   This formula gives a count of branch numbers at the bottom of column D. You use the COUNTA function because the branch numbers are stored as text.

8. **Click Stop Recording on the Developer tab to stop recording the macro.**

   The formatted worksheet should look like something like the one in Figure 1-3.

	A	B	C	D	E	F	G	H	I
1		Region	Market	Branch			Region	Market	Branch
2		NORTH	BUFFALO	601419			SOUTH	CHARLOTTE	173901
3		NORTH	BUFFALO	701407			SOUTH	CHARLOTTE	301301
4		NORTH	BUFFALO	802202			SOUTH	CHARLOTTE	302301
5		NORTH	CANADA	910181			SOUTH	CHARLOTTE	601306
6		NORTH	CANADA	920681			SOUTH	DALLAS	202600
7		NORTH	MICHIGAN	101419			SOUTH	DALLAS	490260
8		NORTH	MICHIGAN	501405			SOUTH	DALLAS	490360
9		NORTH	MICHIGAN	503405			SOUTH	DALLAS	490460
10		NORTH	MICHIGAN	590140			SOUTH	FLORIDA	301316
11		NORTH	NEWYORK	801211			SOUTH	FLORIDA	701309
12		NORTH	NEWYORK	802211			SOUTH	FLORIDA	702309
13		NORTH	NEWYORK	804211			SOUTH	NEWORLEANS	601310
14		NORTH	NEWYORK	805211			SOUTH	NEWORLEANS	602310
15		NORTH	NEWYORK	806211			SOUTH	NEWORLEANS	801607
16	Total			14					

Figure 1-3: Your post-totaled worksheet.

To see your macro in action, delete the Total row you just added and play back your macro by following these steps:

1. **On the Developer tab, select Macros.**

2. **Find and select the AddTotal macro you just recorded.**

3. **Click the Run button.**

If all goes well, the macro plays back your actions to a T and gives your table a total. Now here's the thing. No matter how hard you try, you can't make the AddTotal macro work on the second table. Why? Because you recorded it as an absolute macro.

To understand what this means, examine the underlying code by selecting Macros on the Developer tab. The Macro dialog box appears, as shown in Figure 1-4.

Select the AddTotal macro and click the Edit button. Visual Basic Editor opens and displays the code that was written when you recorded your macro:

```
Sub AddTotal()

  Range("A16").Select

  ActiveCell.FormulaR1C1 = "Total"

  Range("D16").Select

  ActiveCell.FormulaR1C1 = "=COUNTA(R[-14]C:R[-1]C)"

End Sub
```

Pay particular attention to the two lines of code that select range A16 and range D16. Because the macro was recorded in absolute reference mode, Excel interpreted your range selection as absolute cell references. In other words, no matter where your cursor is in your workbook, when you run the recorded macro, Excel will select cell A16 and then cell D16. In the next section, you take a look at what the same macro looks like when recorded in relative reference mode.

Recording macros with relative references

A *relative reference* means relative to the currently active cell. So use caution with your active cell choice — both when you record the relative reference macro and when you run it.

First, make sure the Chapter 1 Sample File.xlsx file is open. (This file is available on this book's companion website at www.dummies.com/extras/excelmacros.) Then, use the following steps to record a relative reference macro:

1. **On the Developer tab, select the Use Relative References option, as shown in Figure 1-5.**

Figure 1-5:
Recording a macro with relative references.

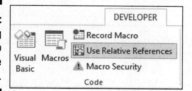

2. **Make sure cell A1 is selected.**

3. **On the Developer tab, select Record Macro.**

4. **Name the macro** AddTotalRelative.

5. **Choose This Workbook for the save location.**

6. **Click OK to start recording.**

7. **Select cell A16 and type** Total **in the cell.**

8. **Select the first empty cell in Column D (D16) and type** = COUNTA(D2:D15).

9. **On the Developer tab, click Stop Recording to stop recording the macro.**

At this point, you've recorded two macros. Take a moment to examine the code for your newly created macro by selecting Macros on the Developer tab to open the Macro dialog box. Choose the AddTotalRelative macro and click Edit.

Again, Visual Basic Editor opens and shows you the code that was written
when you recorded your macro. This time, your code looks something like
the following:

```
Sub AddTotalRelative()

    ActiveCell.Offset(15, 0).Range("A1").Select

    ActiveCell.FormulaR1C1 = "Total"

    ActiveCell.Offset(0, 3).Range("A1").Select

    ActiveCell.FormulaR1C1 = "=COUNTA(R[-14]C:R[-1]C)"

End Sub
```

First note that the code does not contain references to specific cell ranges
(other than the starting point, A1). Note that in this macro, Excel uses the
Offset property of the active cell. This property tells the cursor to move a
certain number of cells up or down and a certain number of cells left or right.

In this case, the Offset property code tells Excel to move 15 rows down and
0 columns across from the active cell (A1). Because the macro was recorded
using relative reference, Excel will not explicitly select a particular cell as it
did when recording an absolute reference macro.

To see this macro in action, delete the Total row for both tables and do the
following:

1. **Select cell A1.**

2. **On the Developer tab, select Macros.**

3. **Find and select the AddTotalRelative macro.**

4. **Click the Run button.**

5. **Select cell F1.**

6. **On the Developer tab, select Macros.**

7. **Find and select the AddTotalRelative macro.**

8. **Click the Run button.**

Note that this macro, unlike your previous macro, works on both sets of data.
Because the macro applies the totals relative to the currently active cell, the
totals are applied correctly.

For this macro to work, you simply need to ensure that

- ✔ You've selected the correct starting cell before running the macro.
- ✔ The block of data has the same number of rows and columns as the data on which you recorded the macro.

I hope this simple example has given you a firm grasp of macro recording with both absolute and relative references.

Other Macro Recording Concepts

At this point, you should feel comfortable recording your own Excel macros. In this section, I describe some other important concepts you'll need to keep in mind when working with macros.

Macro-enabled file extensions

Beginning with Excel 2007, Excel workbooks were given the standard file extension .xlsx. Files with the .xlsx extension cannot contain macros. If your workbook contains macros and you then save that workbook as an .xlsx file, your macros are removed automatically. Excel warns you that macro content will be disabled when saving a workbook with macros as an .xlsx file.

If you want to retain the macros, you must save your file as an Excel macro-enabled workbook. This gives your file an .xlsm extension. The idea is that all workbooks with an .xlsx file extension are automatically known to be safe, whereas you can recognize .xlsm files as a potential threat.

Macro security in Excel 2010

With the release of Office 2010, Microsoft introduced significant changes to its Office security model. One of the most significant changes is the concept of trusted documents. Without getting into the technical minutia, a *trusted document* is essentially a workbook you have deemed to be safe.

If you open a workbook that contains macros in Excel 2010 or later, you see a yellow bar message under the ribbon stating that macros (active content) have been disabled.

If you click Enable, the workbook automatically becomes a trusted document. This means you no longer are prompted to enable the content as long as you open that file on your computer. The basic idea is that if you tell Excel that you trust a particular workbook by enabling macros, it is highly likely that you will enable macros each time you open the workbook. Thus, Excel remembers that you've enabled macros before and inhibits any further messages about macros for that workbook.

This feature is great news for you and your clients. After enabling your macros one time, they won't be annoyed at the constant messages about macros, and you won't have to worry that your macro-enabled dashboard will fall flat because macros have been disabled.

Any workbook you create from scratch will automatically be considered to be trusted. That is, Excel will not require you to enable macros in the workbooks you create.

Trusted locations

If the thought of any macro message coming up (even one time) unnerves you, set up a trusted location for your files. A *trusted location* is a directory that is deemed a safe zone where only trusted workbooks are placed. A trusted location allows you and your clients to run a macro-enabled workbook with no security restrictions as long as the workbook is in that location.

To set up a trusted location, follow these steps:

1. **On the Developer tab, select the Macro Security button.**

   This activates the Trust Center dialog box.

2. **On the left, click Trusted Locations.**

   The Trusted Locations menu appears (see Figure 1-6), displaying all the directories that are considered trusted.

3. **Click the Add New Location button.**

4. **Click Browse, and find and select the directory that will be considered a trusted location.**

After you specify a trusted location, any Excel file that is opened from this location will have macros automatically enabled.

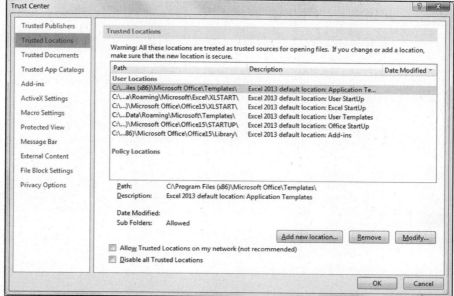

Figure 1-6:
Add
directories
that are
considered
trusted.

Storing macros in your personal macro workbook

Most user-created macros are designed for use in a specific workbook, but you may want to use some macros in all your work. You can store these general-purpose macros in the personal macro workbook so that they're always available to you. The personal macro workbook is loaded whenever you start Excel. This file, named personal.xlsb, doesn't exist until you record a macro using the personal macro workbook as the destination.

To record the macro in your personal macro workbook, select the Personal Macro Workbook option in the Record Macro dialog box before you start recording. This option is in the Store Macro In drop-down list (refer to Figure 1-1).

If you store macros in the personal macro workbook, you don't have to remember to open the personal macro workbook when you load a workbook that uses macros. When you want to exit, Excel asks whether you want to save changes to the personal macro workbook.

The personal macro workbook normally is in a hidden window to keep it out of the way.

Assigning a macro to a button and other form controls

When you create macros, you may want to have a clear and easy way to run each one. A basic button can provide a simple but effective user interface.

As luck would have it, Excel offers a set of form controls for creating user interfaces directly on spreadsheets. Several types of form controls are available, from buttons (the most commonly used control) to scrollbars.

The idea behind using a form control is simple. You place a form control on a spreadsheet and then assign a macro to it — that is, a macro you've already recorded. When the control is clicked, the macro is executed, or played.

Take a moment to create a button for the AddTotalRelative macro you created earlier. Here's how:

1. **On the Developer tab, click the Insert command, shown in Figure 1-7.**

2. **In the drop-down list that appears, select the button form control.**

3. **Click the location where you want to place your button.**

   When you drop the button control on your spreadsheet, the Assign Macro dialog box appears, as shown in Figure 1-8.

4. **Select the macro you want to assign to the button and then click OK.**

At this point, you have a button that runs your macro when you click it! Keep in mind that all controls in the Form Controls group (refer to Figure 1-7) work in the same way as the button form control used in this example. That is to say, you assign a macro to run when the control is selected.

Figure 1-7:
Form
controls
are on the
Developer
tab.

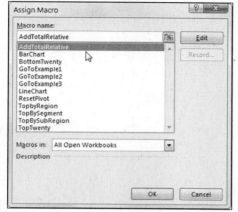

Figure 1-8:
Assign a
macro to the
button.

Placing a macro on the Quick Access toolbar

You can assign a macro not only to a form control on a spreadsheet but also to a button in Excel's Quick Access toolbar. The Quick Access toolbar sits either above or below the ribbon. You can add a custom button that will run your macro by following these steps:

1. **Right-click your Quick Access toolbar and select Customize Quick Access Toolbar.**

   The dialog box illustrated in Figure 1-9 appears.

2. **On the left of the dialog box, click Quick Access Toolbar.**

3. **In the Choose Commands From drop-down list, select Macros.**

4. **Select the macro you want to add and then click the Add button.**

5. **Change the icon by clicking the Modify button.**

Form controls versus ActiveX controls

Note the form controls and ActiveX controls in Figure 1-7. Although they look similar, they're quite different. Form controls are designed for use on a spreadsheet, and ActiveX controls are typically used on Excel user forms. As a general rule, you should always use form controls when working on a spreadsheet. Why? Form controls need less overhead, so they perform better, and configuring form controls is far easier than configuring their ActiveX counterparts.

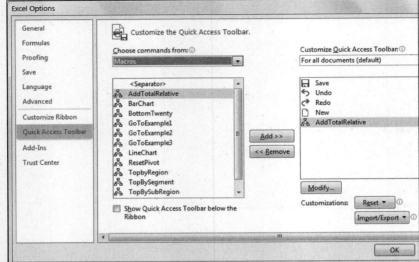

Figure 1-9:
Adding a
macro to
the Quick
Access
toolbar.

Examples of Macros in Action

Covering the fundamentals of building and using macros is one thing. Coming up with good ways to incorporate them in your reporting processes is another. In this section, you take a moment to review a few examples of how macros automate simple reporting tasks.

To follow along in this section, go to www.dummies.com/extras/excel macros and open the Chapter 1 Sample.xlsm file.

Building navigation buttons

The most common use of macros is in navigation. Workbooks that have many worksheets or tabs can be frustrating to navigate. To help your audience, you can create a switchboard, like the one shown in Figure 1-10. When users click the Example 1 button, for example, they're taken to the Example 1 sheet.

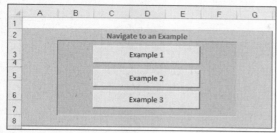

Figure 1-10:
Use macros
to build
buttons
that help
users navi-
gate your
reports.

Creating a macro to navigate to a sheet is quite simple:

1. **Start at the sheet that will become your starting point.**

2. **Start recording a macro.**

3. **While recording, click the destination sheet (the sheet this macro will navigate to).**

4. **Stop recording.**

5. **Add a button form control on your starting point and Assign the macro to a button by selecting your newly recorded macro in the Assign Macro dialog box.**

Excel has a built-in hyperlink feature, which enables you to convert the contents of a cell to a hyperlink that links to another location. That location can be a separate Excel workbook, a website, or another tab in the current workbook. Although creating a hyperlink may be easier than setting up a macro, you can't apply a hyperlink to a form control (such as a button). Instead of a button, you use text to let users know where they'll go when they click the link.

Dynamically rearranging pivot table data

In the example illustrated in Figure 1-11, macros allow a user to change the perspective of the chart simply by selecting one of the buttons shown.

Figure 1-12 reveals that the chart is actually a pivot chart tied to a pivot table. The recorded macros assigned to the buttons do nothing more than rearrange the pivot table to slice the data using various pivot fields.

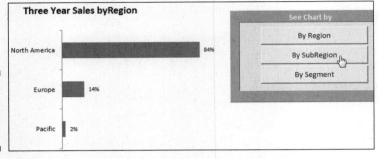

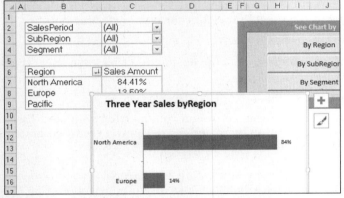

Figure 1-12:
The macros
behind the
buttons
rearrange
the data
fields in a
pivot table.

Here are the high-level steps needed to create this type of setup:

1. **Create your pivot table and a pivot chart.**

2. **Start recording a macro.**

3. **Move a pivot field from one area of the pivot table to the other, and then stop recording the macro.**

4. **Record another macro to move the data field back to its original position.**

5. **Assign each macro to a separate button.**

You can fire your new macros in turn to see your pivot field dynamically move back and forth.

Offering one-touch reporting options

The last two examples demonstrate that you can record any action that you find of value. That is, if you think users would appreciate a certain feature being automated for them, why not record a macro to do so?

In Figure 1-13, note that users can filter the pivot table for the top or bottom 20 customers. Because the steps for this filter have been recorded, users save time and effort and can benefit from this functionality without having to know the steps involved. Also, recording a specific action enables you to manage risk because your users will interact with your reports in a method that you've developed and tested.

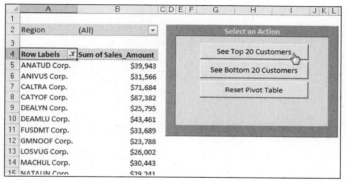

Figure 1-13: Prerecorded views let users benefit from advanced features.

Figure 1-14 demonstrates how you can give your audience a quick and easy way to see the same data on different charts. Don't laugh too quickly at the apparent uselessness of this example. It's not uncommon to be asked to see the same data different ways.

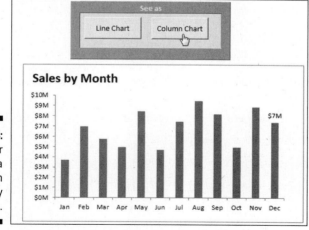

Figure 1-14: Give your users a choice in how they view data.

Instead of taking up real estate with multiple charts, just record a macro that changes the chart type. Your clients will be able to switch views to their heart's content.

Chapter 2

Getting Cozy with Visual Basic Editor

*V*isual Basic Editor (VBE) is the environment where all Excel macros are stored and processed. Each workbook you create comes with this interconnected VBE environment free of charge. Even if you never record one macro, VBE is in the background waiting to be used. When you create a macro, VBE quietly comes to life ready to process the various procedures and routines you give it.

In this chapter, you take your first look behind the curtain to explore Visual Basic Editor.

Working in Visual Basic Editor

Visual Basic Editor is a separate application that runs when you open Excel. To see this hidden VBE environment, you'll need to activate it. The quickest way to activate VBE is to press Alt+F11 when Excel is active. To return to Excel, press Alt+F11 again.

You can activate VBE also by using the Visual Basic command, which is on Excel's Developer tab.

Understanding VBE components

Figure 2-1 shows the VBE program with some of the key parts identified. VBE contains several windows and is highly customizable, so chances are your window won't look exactly like what you see in the figure. You can hide windows, rearrange windows, dock windows, and so on.

Menu bar

The VBE *menu bar* works just like every other menu bar you've encountered. It contains commands that you use to do things with the various components in VBE. Many menu commands have shortcut keys associated with them.

VBE also features shortcut menus. You can right-click almost anything in VBE and get a shortcut menu of common commands.

Toolbar

The *standard toolbar,* which is directly under the menu bar by default, is one of four VBE toolbars. You can customize the toolbars, move them around, display other toolbars, and so on. If you're so inclined, use the

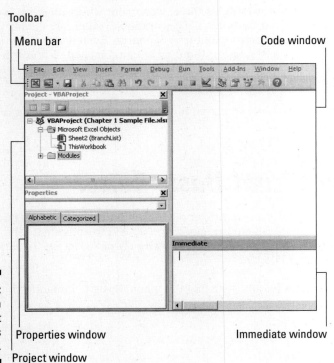

Figure 2-1:
VBE with
significant
elements
identified.

View➪Toolbars command to work with VBE toolbars. Most people just leave them as they are.

Project window

The *project window* displays a tree diagram that shows every workbook currently open in Excel (including add-ins and hidden workbooks). Double-click items to expand or contract them. You'll explore this window in more detail in the "Working with the Project Window" section, later in the chapter.

If the project window is not visible, press Ctrl+R or choose View➪Project Explorer. To hide the project window, click the close button (the X) in its title bar. Alternatively, right-click anywhere in the project window and select Hide from the shortcut menu.

Code window

Every object in a project has an associated *code window,* which contains VBA code. To view an object's code window, double-click the object in the project window. For example, to view the code window for the Sheet1 object, double-click Sheet1 in the project window. Unless you've added some VBA code, the code window will be empty.

You find out more about code windows later in the chapter in the "Working with a Code Window" section.

Immediate window

The *immediate window* may or may not be visible. If it isn't visible, press Ctrl+G or choose View➪Immediate Window. To close the Immediate window, click the close button (the X) in its title bar (or right-click anywhere in the Immediate window and select Hide from the shortcut menu).

The Immediate window is most useful for executing VBA statements directly and for debugging your code. If you're just starting out with VBA, this window won't be that useful, so feel free to hide it and free up some screen space for other things.

Working with the Project Window

When you're working in VBE, each open Excel workbook is a project. You can think of a project as a collection of objects arranged as an outline. You can expand a project by clicking the plus sign (+) at the left of the project's name in the project window. Contract a project by clicking the minus sign (–) to the left of a project's name. Or you can double-click the items to expand and contract them.

Figure 2-2 shows a project window with two projects: a workbook named Book1 and a workbook named Book2, expanded to display their objects.

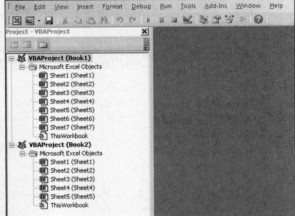

Figure 2-2:
This project
window
lists two
projects.

Every project expands to show at least the Microsoft Excel Objects node. You can expand this node to display an item for each sheet in the workbook (each sheet is considered an object) and another object called ThisWorkbook (which represents the Workbook object). If the project has any VBA modules, the project listing also displays a Modules node.

Adding a new VBA module

When you record a macro, Excel automatically inserts a VBA module to hold the recorded code. The workbook that holds the module for the recorded macro depends on where you chose to store the recorded macro, just before you started recording.

In general, a VBA module can hold three types of code:

- **Declarations:** One or more information statements that you provide to VBA. For example, you can declare the data type for variables you plan to use or set some other module-wide options.

- **Sub procedures:** A set of programming instructions that performs some action. All recorded macros are Sub procedures.

- **Function procedures:** A set of programming instructions that returns a single value (similar in concept to a worksheet function, such as Sum).

A single VBA module can store any number of Sub procedures, Function procedures, and declarations. How you organize a VBA module is up to you. Some people prefer to keep all their VBA code for an application in a single VBA module; others like to split up the code into several modules. It's a personal choice, like arranging furniture.

Follow these steps to manually add a new VBA module to a project:

1. In the project window, select the project's name.

2. Choose Insert⇨Module.

Or you can

1. Right-click the project's name.

2. Choose Insert⇨Module from the shortcut menu.

The new module is added to a Modules folder in the project window (see Figure 2-3). Any modules you create in a given workbook are placed in this Modules folder.

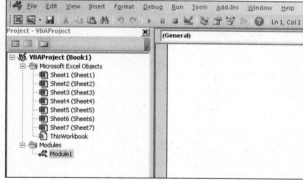

Figure 2-3: Code modules are visible in the Modules folder in the project window.

Removing a VBA module

You may want to remove a code module that is no longer needed. To do so, follow these steps:

1. In the project window, select the module's name.

2. Choose File⇨Remove *xxx*, where *xxx* is the module name.

Or

1. **Right-click the module's name.**
2. **Choose Remove *xxx* from the shortcut menu.**

You can remove VBA modules, but there is no way to remove the other code modules, those for Sheet objects or ThisWorkbook.

Working with a Code Window

As you become proficient with VBA, you'll spend lots of time working in code windows. Macros that you record are stored in a module, and you can type VBA code directly into a VBA module.

Minimizing and maximizing windows

Code windows are much like workbook windows in Excel. You can minimize, maximize, resize, hide, and rearrange them, and more. Most people maximize the code window that they're working on so that they can see more code and reduce distractions.

To maximize a code window, click the maximize button in its title bar (right next to the X) or double-click the title bar. To restore a code window to its original size, click the restore button (the icon that looks like a box) located next to the X.

Sometimes, you may want to have two or more code windows visible. For example, you may want to compare the code in two modules or copy code from one module to another. You can arrange the windows manually, or use the Window⇨Tile Horizontally or Window⇨Tile Vertically command to arrange them automatically.

You can quickly switch among code windows by pressing Ctrl+Tab. If you repeat that key combination, you keep cycling through all open code windows. Pressing Ctrl+Shift+Tab cycles through the windows in reverse order.

Minimizing a code window gets it out of the way. You can also click the close button (the X) in a code window's title bar to close the window completely. (Closing a window just hides it; you won't lose anything). To open it again, just double-click the appropriate object in the project window. Working with these code windows sounds more difficult than it really is.

Getting VBA code into a module

Before you can do anything meaningful, you must have some VBA code in the VBA module. You can get VBA code into a VBA module in three ways:

- ✔ Use the Excel macro recorder to record your actions and convert them to VBA code.
- ✔ Enter the code directly.
- ✔ Copy the code from one module and paste it into another.

You have discovered the excellent method for creating code by using the Excel Macro recorder. However, not all tasks can be translated to VBA by recording a macro. You often have to enter your code directly into the module, either by typing the code by or copying and pasting code you've found elsewhere.

Entering and editing text in a VBA module works as you might expect. You can select, copy, cut, paste, and do other things to the text.

A single line of VBA code can be as long as you like. However, you may want to use the *line-continuation character* to break up lengthy lines of code. To continue a single line of code (also known as a *statement*) from one line to the next, end the first line with a space followed by an underscore (_). Then continue the statement on the next line. Here's an example of a single statement split into three lines:

```
Selection.Sort Key1:=Range("A1"), _

Order1:=xlAscending, Header:=xlGuess, _

Orientation:=xlTopToBottom
```

This statement would perform the same way if it were entered in a single line (with no line-continuation characters).

VBE has multiple levels of undo and redo. If you deleted a statement that you shouldn't have, use the Undo button on the toolbar (or press Ctrl+Z) until the statement appears again. After undoing, you can use the Redo button to perform the changes you've undone.

Ready to enter some real, live code? Try the following steps:

1. **Create a new workbook in Excel.**
2. **Press Alt+F11 to activate VBE.**
3. **Click the new workbook's name in the project window.**
4. **Choose Insert⇨Module to insert a VBA module into the project.**

5. Type the following code into the module:

```
Sub GuessName()

    Dim Msg as String

    Dim Ans As Long

    Msg = "Is your name " & Application.UserName & "?"

    Ans = MsgBox(Msg, vbYesNo)

    If Ans = vbNo Then MsgBox "Oh, never mind."

    If Ans = vbYes Then MsgBox "I must be clairvoyant!"

End Sub
```

6. Make sure the cursor is located anywhere within the text you typed, and then press F5 to execute the procedure.

F5 is a shortcut for the Run➪Run Sub/UserForm command.

When you enter the code listed in step 5, you might notice that VBE makes some adjustments to the text you enter. For example, after you type the Sub statement, VBE automatically inserts the End Sub statement. And if you omit the space before or after an equal sign, VBE inserts the space for you. Also, VBE changes the color and capitalization of some text. These changes are VBE's way of keeping things neat and readable.

If you followed the previous steps, you just created a VBA Sub procedure, also known as a macro. When you press F5, Excel executes the code and follows the instructions. In other words, Excel evaluates each statement and does what you told it to do. You can execute this macro any number of times — although it tends to lose its appeal after a few dozen executions.

This simple macro uses the following concepts:

- Defining a Sub procedure (the first line)
- Declaring variables (the Dim statements)
- Assigning values to variables (Msg and Ans)
- Concatenating (joining) a string (using the & operator)
- Using a built-in VBA function (MsgBox)
- Using built-in VBA constants (vbYesNo, vbNo, and vbYes)
- Using an If-Then construct (twice)
- Ending a Sub procedure (the last line)

As mentioned, you can copy and paste code into a VBA module. For example, a Sub or Function procedure that you write for one project might also be useful in another project. Instead of wasting time reentering the code, you can activate the module and use the normal copy-and-paste procedures (Ctrl+C to copy and Ctrl+V to paste). After pasting the code into a VBA module, you can modify the code as necessary.

Customizing the VBA Environment

If you're serious about becoming an Excel programmer, you'll spend a lot of time with VBA modules on your screen. To help make things as comfortable as possible, VBE provides quite a few customization options.

When VBE is active, choose Tools➪Options. You'll see a dialog box with four tabs: Editor, Editor Format, General, and Docking. Take a moment to explore some of the options found on each tab.

The Editor tab

Figure 2-4 shows the options accessed by clicking the Editor tab of the Options dialog box. Use the option in the Editor tab to control how certain things work in VBE.

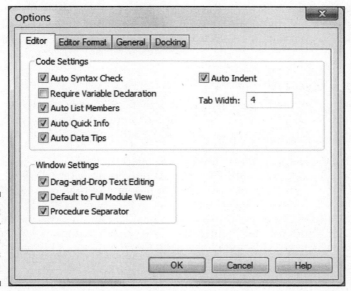

Figure 2-4:
The Editor tab in the Options dialog box.

The Auto Syntax Check option

The Auto Syntax Check setting determines whether VBE pops up a dialog box if it discovers a syntax error while you're entering your VBA code. The dialog box tells roughly what the problem is. If you don't choose this setting, VBE flags syntax errors by displaying them in a different color from the rest of the code, and you don't have to deal with dialog boxes popping up on your screen.

The Require Variable Declaration option

If the Require Variable Declaration option is set, the VBE will insert an Option Explicit statement at the beginning of each new VBA module you add. When the Option Explicit statement appears in your module, you must explicitly define each variable you use. You get a detailed look at variables in Chapter 3.

The Auto List Members option

If the Auto List Members option is set, VBE provides some help when you're entering your VBA code. It displays a list that would logically complete the statement you're typing. This feature is one of the best in VBE.

The Auto Quick Info option

If the Auto Quick Info option is selected, VBE displays information about functions and their arguments as you type. This behavior is similar to the way Excel lists the arguments for a function as you start typing a new formula.

The Auto Data Tips option

If the Auto Data Tips option is set, VBE displays the value of the variable over which your cursor is placed when you're debugging code. This option is turned on by default and is often quite useful. There is no reason to turn off this option.

The Auto Indent setting

The Auto Indent setting determines whether VBE automatically indents each new line of code the same as the preceding line. Most Excel developers are keen on using indentations in their code, so this option is typically kept on.

By the way, use the Tab key, not the spacebar, to indent your code. Also, you can press Shift+Tab to outdent a line of code. If you want to indent more than just one line, select all lines you want to indent and then press the Tab key.

VBE's Edit toolbar (which is hidden by default) contains two useful buttons: Indent and Outdent. These buttons let you quickly indent or outdent a block of code. Select the code and click one of these buttons to change the block's indenting.

The Drag-and-Drop Text Editing option

The Drag-and-Drop Text Editing option, when enabled, lets you copy and move text by dragging and dropping with your mouse.

The Default to Full Module View option

The Default to Full Module View option sets the default state for new modules. (It doesn't affect existing modules.) If set, procedures in the code window appear as a single scrollable list. If this option is turned off, you can see only one procedure at a time.

The Procedure Separator option

When the Procedure Separator option is turned on, separator bars appear at the end of each procedure in a code window. Separator bars provide a nice visual line between procedures, making it easy to see where one piece of code ends and another starts.

The Editor Format tab

Figure 2-5 shows the Editor Format tab of the Options dialog box. With this tab, you can customize the way VBE looks.

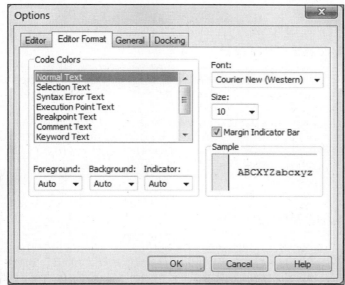

Figure 2-5:
Change VBE's look with the Editor Format tab.

The Code Colors option

The Code Colors option lets you set the text color and background color displayed for various elements of VBA code. Most Excel developers stick with the default colors. But if you like to change things up, play around with these settings.

The Font option

The Font option lets you select the font used in your VBA modules. For best results, stick with a fixed-width font such as Courier New. In a fixed-width font, all characters are the same width. This type of font makes your code easier to read because the characters are nicely aligned vertically. You can also easily distinguish multiple spaces (which is sometimes useful).

The Size setting

The Size setting specifies the point size of the font in the VBA modules. This setting is a matter of personal preference determined by your video display resolution and how good your eyesight is.

The Margin Indicator Bar option

The Margin Indicator Bar option controls the display of the vertical margin indicator bar in your modules. You should keep this option turned on; otherwise, you won't be able to see the helpful graphical indicators when you're debugging your code.

The General tab

Figure 2-6 shows the options available on the General tab in the Options dialog box. In almost every case, the default settings are just fine.

The most important setting on the General tab is Error Trapping. If you are just starting your Excel macro-writing career, it's best to leave Error Trapping set to Break on Unhandled Errors. This setting ensures that Excel can identify errors as you type your code.

The Docking tab

Figure 2-7 shows the Docking tab. Its options determine how the various windows in VBE behave. When a window is docked, it is fixed in place along one edge of the VBE program window. Docking makes it much easier to identify and locate a particular window. If you turn off all docking, you have a big, confusing mess of windows. Generally, the default settings work fine.

Figure 2-6:
The General
tab of the
Options
dialog box.

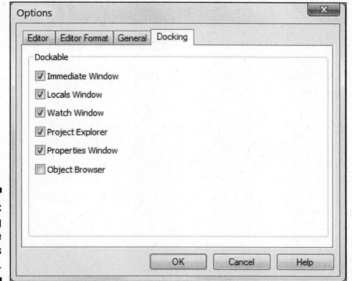

Figure 2-7:
The Docking
tab of the
Options
dialog box.

Chapter 3

The Anatomy of Macros

*T*he engine behind macros is VBA (Visual Basic for Applications). When you record a macro, Excel is busy writing the associated VBA behind the scenes. To fully understand macros, it's important to understand the underlying VBA typically used in Excel macros.

This chapter starts you on that journey by giving you a primer on some of the objects, variables, events, and error handlers you will encounter in the macro examples found in this book.

An Overview of the Excel Object Model

Visual Basic for Applications is an object-oriented programming language. The basic concept of *object-oriented programming* is that a software application (Excel in this case) consists of various individual objects, each of which has its own set of features and uses. An Excel application contains cells, worksheets, charts, pivot tables, drawing shapes — the list of Excel's objects is seemingly endless. Each object has its own set of features, which are called *properties,* and its own set of uses, called *methods.*

You can think of this concept just as you would the objects you encounter every day, such as your computer, car, or refrigerator. Each of these objects has identifying qualities, such as height, weight, and color. They each have their own distinct uses, such as working with Excel, transporting you over long distances, or keeping perishable foods cold.

VBA objects also have identifiable properties and methods of use. A worksheet cell is an object, and among its describable features (its properties) are its address, height, and formatted fill color. A workbook is also a VBA object, and among its usable features (its methods) are its capabilities to be opened, closed, and have a chart or pivot table added to it.

In Excel you deal with workbooks, worksheets, and ranges on a daily basis. You likely think of each of these objects as all part of Excel, not really separating them in your mind. However, Excel thinks about these internally as all part of a hierarchical model called the Excel Object Model. *The Excel Object Model* is a clearly defined set of objects that are structured according to the relationships between them.

Understanding objects

In the real world, you can describe everything you see as an object. When you look at your house, it is an object. Your house has rooms; those rooms are also separate objects. Those rooms may have closets. Those closets are likewise objects. As you think about your house, the rooms, and the closets, you may see a hierarchical relationship between them. Excel works in the same way.

In Excel, the *Application object* is the all-encompassing object — similar to your house. Inside the Application object, Excel has a workbook. Inside a workbook is a worksheet. Inside that is a range. These are all objects that live in a hierarchical structure.

To point to a specific object in VBA, you can traverse the object model. For example, to get to cell A1 on Sheet 1, you can enter this code:

```
Activeworkbook.Sheets("Sheet1").Range("A1").Select
```

In most cases, the object model hierarchy is understood, so you don't have to type every level. Entering this code also gets you to cell A1 because Excel infers that you mean the active workbook, and the active sheet:

```
Range("A1").Select
```

Indeed, if you have your cursor already in cell A1, you can simply use the ActiveCell object, negating the need to spell out the range:

```
Activecell.Select
```

Understanding collections

Many of Excel's objects belong to *collections,* which are essentially groups of like objects. Similarly, your house sits within a neighborhood, which is a collection of houses. Each neighborhood sits in a collection of neighborhoods called a city. Excel considers collections to be objects themselves.

In each Workbook object, you have a collection of Worksheets. The Worksheets collection is an object that you can call upon through VBA. Each worksheet in your workbook lives in the Worksheets collection.

If you want to refer to a worksheet in the Worksheets collection, you can refer to it by its position in the collection, as an index number starting with 1, or by its name, as quoted text. If you run the following two lines of code in a workbook that has only one worksheet called MySheet, they both do the same thing:

```
Worksheets(1).Select

Worksheets("MySheet").Select
```

If you have two worksheets in the active workbook that have the names MySheet and YourSheet, in that order, you can refer to the second worksheet by typing either of these statements:

```
Worksheets(2).Select

Worksheets("YourSheet").Select
```

If you want to refer to a worksheet in a workbook called MySheet in a particular workbook that is not active, you must qualify the worksheet reference and the workbook reference, as follows:

```
Workbooks("MyData.xls").Worksheets("MySheet").Select
```

Understanding properties

Properties are essentially the characteristics of an object. Your house has a color, a square footage, an age, and so on. Some properties, such as the color of your house, can be changed. Other properties, such as the year your house was built, can't be changed.

Likewise, an object in Excel such as the Worksheet object has a sheet name property that can be changed, and a Rows.Count row property that cannot.

You refer to the property of an object by referring to the object and then to the property. For instance, you can change the name of your worksheet by changing its Name property.

In this example, you rename Sheet1 to MySheet:

```
Sheets("Sheet1").Name = "MySheet"
```

Some properties are read-only, which means that you can't assign a value to them directly. An example of a read-only property is the Text property of cell, which provides the formatted appearance of a value in a cell. You cannot overwrite or change it.

Understanding methods

Methods are the actions that can be performed against an object. It helps to think of methods as verbs. For example, you can paint your house; in VBA, that might translate to

```
house.paint
```

A simple example of an Excel method is the Select method of the Range object:

```
Range("A1").Select
```

Another is the Copy method of the Range object:

```
Range("A1").Copy
```

Some methods have parameters that can dictate how the methods are applied. For instance, the Paste method can be used more effectively by explicitly defining the Destination parameter:

```
ActiveSheet.Paste Destination:=Range("B1")
```

A Brief Look at Variables

Another concept you will see throughout the macros in this book is the concept of variables. It's important to dedicate a few words on this concept because it will play a big part in most of the macros you will encounter here.

You can think of *variables* as memory containers that you can use in your procedures. There are different types of variables, each tasked with holding a specific type of data.

Some of the common types of variables you will see in this book follow:

- ✔ String: Holds textual data
- ✔ Integer: Holds numeric data ranging from –32,768 to 32,767
- ✔ Long: Holds numeric data ranging from –2,147,483,648 to 2,147,483,647
- ✔ Double: Holds floating-point numeric data
- ✔ Variant: Holds any kind of data
- ✔ Boolean: Holds binary data that returns True or False
- ✔ Object: Holds an object from the Excel Object model

When you create a variable in a macro, you are *declaring a variable*. You do so by entering Dim (abbreviation for dimension), then the name of your variable, and then the type. For instance:

```
Dim MyText as String

Dim MyNumber as Integer

Dim MyWorksheet as Worksheet
```

After you create your variable, you can fill it with data. Here are a few simple examples of how you could create a variable, and then assign values to it:

```
Dim MyText as String
MyText = Range("A1").Value

Dim MyNumber as Integer
MyNumber = Range("B1").Value * 25

Dim MyObject as Worksheet
Set MyWorksheet = Sheets("Sheet1")
```

The values you assign to your variables often come from data stored in your cells. However, the values may also be information that you create. It all depends on the task at hand. This notion will become clearer as you go through the macros in this book.

Although it's possible to create code that does not use variables, you'll encounter many examples of VBA code where variables *are* employed. There are two main reasons for this.

First, Excel doesn't inherently know what your data is used for. It doesn't see numerals, symbols, or letters. It sees only data. When you declare variables with specific data types, you help Excel know how it should handle certain pieces of data so that your macros will produce the results you'd expect.

Second, variables help by making your code more efficient and easier to understand. For example, suppose you have a number in cell A1 that you are repeatedly referring to in your macro. You could retrieve that number by pointing to cell A1 each time you need it:

```
Sub Macro1()

Range("B1").Value = Range("A1").Value * 5

Range("C1").Value = Range("A1").Value * 10

Range("D1").Value = Range("A1").Value * 15

End Sub
```

However, this macro would force Excel to waste cycles storing the same number in memory every time you point to cell A1. Also, if you need to change your workbook so that the target number is not in cell A1, but in, say, cell A2, you would need to edit your code by changing all the references from A1 to A2.

A better way is to store the number in cell A1 just once. For example, you can store the value in cell A1 in an Integer variable called myValue:

```
Sub WithVariable()

Dim myValue As Integer

myValue = Range("A1").Value

Range("C3").Value = myValue * 5

Range("D5").Value = myValue * 10

Range("E7").Value = myValue * 15

End Sub
```

This approach not only improves the efficiency of your code (ensuring Excel reads the number in cell A1 just once) but also ensures that you only have to edit one line should the design of your workbook change.

Understanding Event Procedures

In many of the example macros in this book, code is implemented as an event procedure. To fully understand why these examples use event procedures, it's important to get acquainted with events.

An *event* is nothing more than an action that takes place during a session in Excel. Everything that happens in Excel happens to an object through an event. A few examples of events are opening a workbook, adding a worksheet, changing a value in a cell, saving a workbook, and double-clicking a cell.

The nifty thing is that you can tell Excel to run a certain macro or piece of code when a particulate event occurs. For example, you may want to ensure that your workbook automatically saves each time it closes. You can add code to the BeforeClose workbook event that saves the workbook before it closes.

In Chapter 2, in the section on adding a new VBA module, you discover how to create a standard VBA module to hold the code you write. However, event procedures are special in that they are not stored in standard modules. As you see in the next few sections, event procedures are stored directly in each object's built-in modules.

Worksheet events

Worksheet events occur when something happens to a particular worksheet, such as when a worksheet is selected, a cell on the worksheet is edited, or a formula on a worksheet is calculated. Each worksheet has its own built-in module where you can place your own event procedure.

To get to this built-in module, you can right-click the worksheet and select the View Code option, as shown in Figure 3-1.

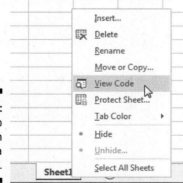

Figure 3-1:
Getting to
the built-in
module for a
worksheet.

Visual Basic Editor will automatically open to the built-in module for the worksheet. At the top of the module are two drop-down boxes.

In the drop-down box on the left, select the Worksheet option. The SelectionChange event in the drop-down box on the right is selected automatically. This action also adds some starter code (see Figure 3-2), where you can enter or paste your code.

Figure 3-2:
The default
Selection
Change
event.

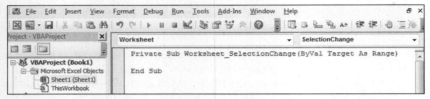

The idea is to choose the most appropriate event from the Event drop-down box for the task at hand. Figure 3-3 illustrates the different events you can choose.

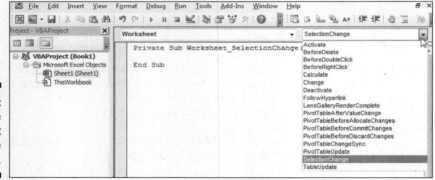

Figure 3-3:
Choose
the most
appropriate
event.

The more commonly used worksheet events follow:

- **Worksheet_Change:** Triggers when any data on the worksheet is changed

- **Worksheet_SelectionChange:** Triggers each time a new cell or an object on the worksheet is selected

- **Worksheet_BeforeDoubleClick:** Triggers before Excel responds to a double-click on the worksheet

- **Worksheet_BeforeRightClick:** Triggers before Excel responds to a right-click on the worksheet
- **Worksheet_Activate:** Triggers when the user moves from another worksheet to this worksheet
- **Worksheet_Deactivate:** Triggers when the user moves from this worksheet to another worksheet
- **Worksheet_Calculate:** Triggers each time a change in the worksheet causes Excel to recalculate formulas

Workbook events

Workbook events occur when something happens to a particular workbook. For example, when a workbook is opened, when a workbook is closed, when a new worksheet is added, or when a workbook is saved. Each workbook is its own built-in module where you can place your own event procedure.

To get to this built-in module, you will need to first activate the Visual Basic Editor (press Alt+F11). Then in the Project Explorer menu, right-click on ThisWorkbook, and then choose the ViewCode option (see Figure 3-4).

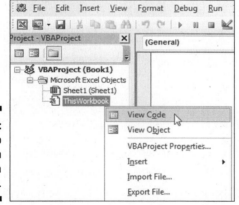

Figure 3-4:
Getting to the built-in module for a workbook.

The Visual Basic Editor will automatically open to the built-in module for the workbook. This module will have two dropdown boxes at the top.

Select the Workbook option in the dropdown on the left. This action will automatically select the Open event in the dropdown on the right. As you can see in Figure 3-5, this will also added some starter code where you can enter or paste your code.

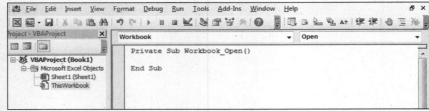

Figure 3-5:
The default
Open event
for the
Worksheet
object.

The idea is to choose the most appropriate event from the Event dropdown for the task at hand. Figure 3-6 illustrates some of the events you can choose.

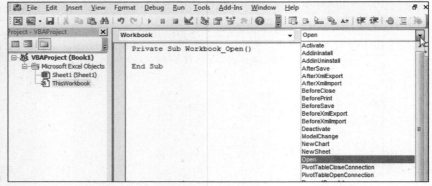

Figure 3-6:
Click the
Event drop-
down box
to choose
the most
appropriate
event.

The more commonly used workbook events are as follows:

- ✔ **Worksheet_Open:** Triggers when the workbook is opened
- ✔ **Worksheet_BeforeSave:** Triggers before the workbook is saved
- ✔ **Worksheet_BeforeClose:** Triggers before Excel closes the workbook
- ✔ **Worksheet_SheetChange:** Triggers when a user switches between sheets

Error Handling in a Nutshell

In some of the macros in this book, you'll see a line similar to this:

```
On Error GoTo MyError
```

This is called an error handler. *Error handlers* allow you to specify what happens when an error is encountered while your code runs.

Without error handlers, any error that occurs in your code will prompt Excel to activate a less-than-helpful error message that typically won't clearly convey what happened. However, with the aid of error handlers, you can choose to ignore the error or exit the code gracefully with your own message to the user.

There are three types of On Error statements:

- **On Error GoTo SomeLabel:** The code jumps to the specified label.
- **On Error Resume Next:** The error is ignored and the code resumes.
- **On Error GoTo 0:** VBA resets to normal error-checking behavior.

On Error GoTo SomeLabel

Sometimes an error in your code means you need to gracefully exit the procedure and give your users a clear message. In these situations, you can use the On Error GoTo statement to tell Excel to jump to a certain line of code.

For example, in the following small piece of code, you tell Excel to divide the value in cell A1 by the value in cell A2, and then place the answer in cell A3. Easy. What could go wrong?

```
Sub Macro1()

Range("A3").Value = Range("A1").Value / Range("A2").Value

End Sub
```

As it turns out, two major things can go wrong. If cell A2 contains 0, you get a divide by 0 error. If cell A2 contains a non-numeric value, you get a type mismatch error.

To avoid a nasty error message, you can tell Excel that On Error, you want the code execution to jump to the label called MyExit.

In the following code, the MyExit label is followed by a message to the user that gives friendly advice instead of a nasty error message. Also note the Exit Sub line before the MyExit label, which ensures that the code will simply exit if no error is encountered:

```
Sub Macro1()

On Error GoTo MyExit

Range("A3").Value = Range("A1").Value / Range("A2").Value
Exit Sub

MyExit:
MsgBox "Please Use Valid Non-Zero Numbers"

End Sub
```

On Error Resume Next

Sometimes, you want Excel to ignore an error and simply resume running the code. In these situations, you can use the On Error Resume Next statement.

For example, the following piece of code is meant to delete a file called GhostFile.exe from the C:\Temp directory. After the file is deleted, a nice message box tells the user that the file is gone:

```
Sub Macro1()

Kill "C:\Temp\GhostFile.exe"

MsgBox "File has been deleted."

End Sub
```

The code works great if there is indeed a file to delete. But if for some reason the file called GhostFile.exe does not exist in the C:\Temp drive, an error is thrown.

In this case, you don't care if the file is not there because you were going to delete it anyway. So you can simply ignore the error and move on with the code.

By using the On Error Resume Next statement, the code runs its course whether or not the targeted file exists:

```
Sub Macro1()

On Error Resume Next
```

```
Kill "C:\Temp\GhostFile.exe"

MsgBox "File has been deleted."

End Sub
```

On Error GoTo 0

When using certain error statements, it may be necessary to reset the error-checking behavior of VBA. To understand what this means, take a look at the next example.

Here, you first want to delete a file called GhostFile.exe from the C:\Temp directory. To avoid errors that may stem from the fact that the targeted file does not exist, you use the On Error Resume Next statement. After that, you try to do some suspect math by dividing 100/Mike:

```
Sub Macro1()

On Error Resume Next

Kill "C:\Temp\GhostFile.exe"

Range("A3").Value = 100 / "Mike"

End Sub
```

Running this piece of code should generate an error due to the fuzzy math, but it doesn't. Why? Because the last instruction you gave to the code was On Error Resume Next. Any error encountered after that line is effectively ignored.

To remedy this problem, you can use the On Error GoTo 0 statement to resume normal error-checking behavior:

```
Sub Macro1()

On Error Resume Next

Kill "C:\Temp\GhostFile.exe"

On Error GoTo 0

Range("A3").Value = 100 / "Mike"

End Sub
```

This code will ignore errors until the On Error GoTo 0 statement. After that statement, the code goes back to normal error checking and triggers the expected error stemming from the fuzzy math.

Part II
Making Short Work of Workbook Tasks

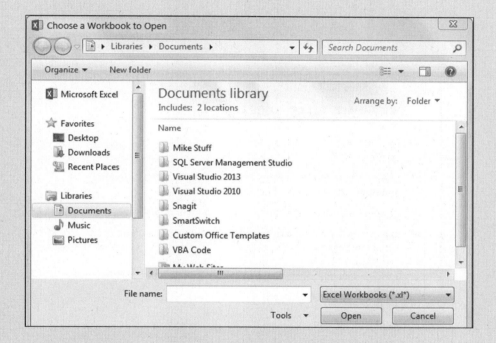

See the article at www.dummies.com/extras/excelmacros to uncover a technique that will force your clients to enable the macros in your workbooks.

In this part . . .

- ✔ Look at various techniques you can use to manipulate your workbooks.

- ✔ See how you can leverage macros to automate the creation and duplication of Excel files.

- ✔ Uncover macros that automate common worksheet tasks.

- ✔ Explore how you can use macros to protect and back up your Excel workbooks.

Chapter 4

Working with Workbooks

A workbook is not just an Excel file; it's also an object in Excel's *Object model* (a programming hierarchy that exposes parts of Excel to VBA).

You can reference workbooks through VBA to do cool things like automatically create new workbooks, prevent users from closing workbooks, and automatically back up workbooks. In this chapter, you explore a few of the more useful workbook-related macros.

Creating a Workbook from Scratch

You may sometimes want or need to create a workbook in an automated way. For instance, you may need to copy data from a table and paste it into a newly created workbook. The following macro copies a range of cells from the active sheet and pastes the data into a new workbook.

How the macro works

As you'll see when you read through the lines of the code, this macro is relatively intuitive:

```
Sub Macro1()

'Step 1 Copy the data
    Sheets("Example 1").Range("B4:C15").Copy

'Step 2 Create a new workbook
    Workbooks.Add

'Step 3 Paste the data
    ActiveSheet.Paste Destination:=Range("A1")

'Step 4 Turn off application alerts
    Application.DisplayAlerts = False

'Step 5 Save the newly created workbook
    ActiveWorkbook.SaveAs _
    Filename:="C:\Temp\MyNewBook.xlsx"

'Step 6 Turn application alerts back on
    Application.DisplayAlerts = True

End Sub
```

In Step 1, you simply copy the data that ranges from cells B4 to C15. Note that you specify both the sheet and the range by name. This approach is a best practice when working with multiple open workbooks.

In Step 2, you use the Add method of the Workbook object to create a workbook. The blank workbook is equivalent to manually choosing File ⇨ New ⇨ Blank Document in the Excel ribbon.

In Step 3, you use the Paste method to send the copied data to cell A1 of the new workbook.

Pay attention to the fact that the code refers to the ActiveSheet object. When you add a workbook, the new workbook immediately gains focus, becoming the active workbook. (Excel does the same when you add a workbook manually.)

In Step 4 of the code, you set the DisplayAlerts method to False, effectively turning off Excel's warnings. You do this because in the next step of the code, you save the newly created workbook. You may run this macro multiple times, in which case Excel attempts to save the file multiple times.

What happens when you try to save a workbook multiple times? That's right — Excel warns you that there is already a file with that name and then asks if you want to overwrite the previously existing file. Because your goal is to automate the creation of the workbook, you want to suppress that warning.

In Step 5, you save the file by using the SaveAs method. Note that you enter the full path of the save location, including the final filename.

Because you turned off application alters in Step 4, you need to turn them back on (see Step 6). If you don't, Excel continues to suppress all warnings during the current session.

How to use the macro

To implement this macro, you can copy and paste it into a standard module:

1. **Activate Visual Basic Editor by pressing Alt+F11.**
2. **Right-click the project/workbook name in the project window.**
3. **Choose Insert ⇨ Module.**
4. **Type or paste the code in the newly created module.**

   You'll probably need to change the sheet name, the range address, and the save location.

Saving a Workbook when a Particular Cell Is Changed

Sometimes, you may be working on data that is so sensitive that you'll want to save every time a particular cell or range of cells is changed. The next macro allows you to define a range of cells that, when changed, forces the workbook to save.

In the example demonstrated in Figure 4-1, you want the workbook to save when an edit is made to any of the cells in the range C5:C16.

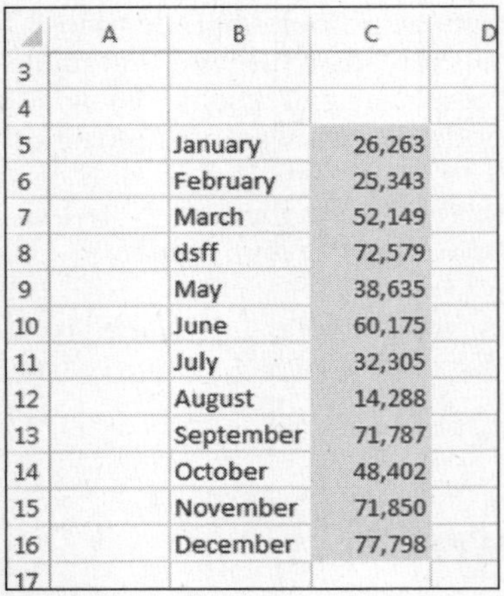

	A	B	C	D
3				
4				
5		January	26,263	
6		February	25,343	
7		March	52,149	
8		dsff	72,579	
9		May	38,635	
10		June	60,175	
11		July	32,305	
12		August	14,288	
13		September	71,787	
14		October	48,402	
15		November	71,850	
16		December	77,798	
17				

Figure 4-1: Changing a cell in C5:C16 forces the workbook to save.

How the macro works

The secret to this code is the Intersect method. Because you don't want to save the worksheet when any old cell changes, you use the Intersect method to determine if the target cell (the cell that changed) intersects with the range specified as the trigger range (C5:C16 in this case).

The Intersect method returns one of two things: a Range object that defines the intersection between the two given ranges, or nothing. So in essence, you need to throw the target cell against the Intersect method to check for a value of Nothing. At that point, you can decide whether to save the workbook.

```
Private Sub Worksheet_Change(ByVal Target As Range)

'Step 1: Does the changed range intersect?
    If Intersect(Target, Range("C5:C16")) Is Nothing Then

'Step 2: If there is no intersection, exit procedure
    Exit Sub

'Step 3: If there is an intersection, save the workbook
    Else
    ActiveWorkbook.Save

'Step 4: Close out the If statement
    End If

End Sub
```

In Step 1, you simply check to see whether the target cell (the cell that has changed) is in the range specified by the Intersect method. A value of Nothing means the target cell is outside the range specified.

Step 2 forces the macro to stop and exit the procedure if there is no intersection between the target cell and the specified range.

If there is an intersection, Step 3 fires the Save method of the active workbook, overwriting the previous version.

In Step 4, you simply close out the If statement. Every time you start an If-Then-Else check, you must close it out with a corresponding End If.

How to use the macro

To implement this macro, you need to copy and paste it into the Worksheet_ Change event code window. Placing the macro here allows it to run each time you make any change to the sheet:

1. **Activate Visual Basic Editor by pressing Alt+F11.**

2. **In the project window, find your project/workbook name and click the plus sign next to it to see all the sheets.**

3. **Click the sheet from which you want to trigger the code.**

4. **In the Event drop-down list (see Figure 4-2), select the Change event.**

5. **Type or paste the code in the newly created module, changing the range address to suit your needs.**

Figure 4-2:
Enter your code in the Worksheet Change event.

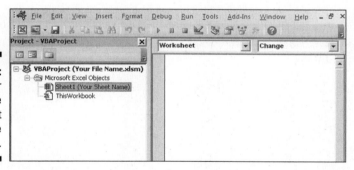

Saving a Workbook before Closing

The macro presented in this section is an excellent way to protect users from inadvertently closing their file before saving. When implemented, this macro ensures that Excel automatically saves the workbook before closing it.

Excel will normally warn users who are attempting to close an unsaved workbook, giving them an option to save before closing. However, many users may blow past the warning and inadvertently click No, telling Excel to close without saving. With this macro, you are protecting against this by automatically saving before closing.

How the macro works

The code is triggered by the workbook's BeforeClose event. When you try to close the workbook, this event fires, running the code within. The crux of the code is simple — it asks the users whether they want to close the workbook (see Figure 4-3). The macro then evaluates whether the user clicked OK or Cancel.

Figure 4-3:
The message you see when you try to close the workbook.

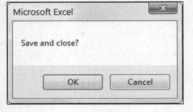

The evaluation is done with a Select Case statement. The Select Case statement is an alternative to the If-Then-Else statement, allowing you to perform condition checks in your macros. The basic construct of a Select Case statement is simple:

```
Select Case <some expression to check>
Case Is = <some value>
     <do something>
Case Is=<some other value>
     <do something else>
Case Is=<some 3rd value>
     <do some 3rd thing>
End Select
```

With a Select Case statement, you can perform many conditional checks. In this case, you are simply checking for OK or Cancel. Take a look at the code:

```
Private Sub Workbook_BeforeClose(Cancel As Boolean)

'Step 1: Activate the message box and start the check
    Select Case MsgBox("Save and close?", vbOKCancel)
```

```
'Step 2: Cancel button pressed, so cancel the close
    Case Is = vbCancel
    Cancel = True

'Step 3: OK button pressed, so save the workbook and close
    Case Is = vbOK
    ActiveWorkbook.Save

'Step 4: Close your Select Case statement
End Select

End Sub
```

In Step 1, you activate the message box as the condition check for the Select Case statement. You use vbOKCancel argument to ensure that the OK and Cancel buttons are presented as choices.

In Step 2, if the user clicked Cancel in the message box, the macro tells Excel to cancel the Workbook_Close event by passing True to the Cancel Boolean.

If the user clicked the OK button in the message box, Step 3 takes effect. Here, you tell Excel to save the workbook. And because you didn't set the Cancel Boolean to True, Excel continues with the close.

In Step 4, you simply close out the Select Case statement. Every time you instantiate a Select Case, you must close it out with a corresponding End Select.

How to use the macro

To implement this macro, you need to copy and paste it into the Workbook_ BeforeClose event code window. Placing the macro there allows it to run each time you try to close the workbook:

1. **Activate Visual Basic Editor by pressing Alt+F11.**

2. **In the project window, find your project/workbook name and click the plus sign next to it to see all the sheets.**

3. **Click ThisWorkbook.**

4. **In the Event drop-down list (see Figure 4-4), select the BeforeClose event.**

5. **Type or paste the code in the newly created module.**

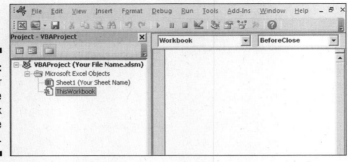

Figure 4-4:
Enter your
code in the
Workbook
BeforeClose
event.

Protecting a Worksheet on Workbook Close

Sometimes you need to send your workbook out into the world with specific worksheets protected. If you find that you're constantly protecting and unprotecting sheets before distributing your workbooks, the macro in this section can help you.

How the macro works

The code is triggered by the workbook's BeforeClose event. When you try to close the workbook, this event fires, running the code within. The macro automatically protects the specified sheet with the given password, and then saves the workbook:

```
Private Sub Workbook_BeforeClose(Cancel As Boolean)

'Step 1: Protect the sheet with a password
    Sheets("Sheet1").Protect Password:="RED"

'Step 2: Save the workbook
    ActiveWorkbook.Save

End Sub
```

In Step 1, you're explicitly specifying which sheet to protect — Sheet1, in this case. You also provide the password argument, Password:="RED", which defines the password needed to remove protection.

This password argument is optional. If you omit it, the sheet will still be protected, but you won't need a password to unprotect it.

Excel passwords are case-sensitive, so you'll want to pay attention to the exact password and capitalization that you are using.

Step 2 tells Excel to save the workbook. If you don't save the workbook, the sheet protection you just applied won't be in effect the next time the workbook is opened.

How to use the macro

To implement this macro, you need to copy and paste it into the Workbook_ BeforeClose event code window. Placing the macro here allows it to run each time you try to close the workbook:

1. **Activate Visual Basic Editor by pressing Alt+F11.**

2. **In the project window, find your project/workbook name and click the plus sign next to it to see all the sheets.**

3. **Click ThisWorkbook.**

4. **In the Event drop-down list (see Figure 4-5), select the BeforeClose event.**

5. **Type or paste the code in the newly created module, modifying the sheet name (if necessary) and the password.**

Note that you can protect additional sheets by adding addition statements before the Activeworkbook.Save statement.

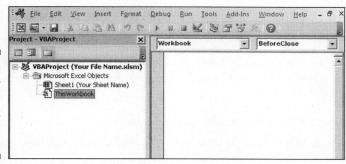

Figure 4-5: Enter your code in the Workbook BeforeClose event.

Unprotecting a Worksheet on Workbook Open

If you've distributed workbooks with protected sheets, you likely get the workbooks back with the sheets still protected. Often, you need to unprotect the worksheets in a workbook before continuing your work. If you find that you are continuously unprotecting worksheets, this section's macro may be just the ticket.

How the macro works

The code is triggered by the workbook's Open event. When you open a workbook, this event triggers, running the code within. This macro automatically unprotects the specified sheet with the given password when the workbook is opened:

```
Private Sub Workbook_Open()

'Step 1: Protect the sheet with a password
    Sheets("Sheet1").Unprotect Password:="RED"

End Sub
```

The macro explicitly names the sheet you want to unprotect — Sheet1, in this case. Then it passes the password required to unprotect the sheet.

Excel passwords are case-sensitive, so pay attention to the exact password and capitalization that you are using.

How to use the macro

To implement this macro, you need to copy and paste it into the Workbook_Open event code window. Placing the macro here allows it to run each time the workbook is opened:

1. **Activate Visual Basic Editor by pressing Alt+F11.**

2. **In the project window, find your project/workbook name and click the plus sign next to it to see all the sheets.**

3. **Click ThisWorkbook.**

4. **In the Event drop-down list (see Figure 4-6), select the Open event.**

5. **Type or paste the code in the newly created module, modifying the sheet name (if necessary) and the password.**

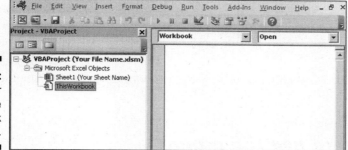

Figure 4-6:
Enter your code in the Workbook Open event.

Opening a Workbook to a Specific Tab

In some situations, it's imperative that your workbook be started on a specific worksheet. With the next macro, if users are working with your workbook, they can't go astray because the workbook starts on the exact worksheet it needs to.

In the example illustrated in Figure 4-7, you want the workbook to go immediately to the sheet called Start Here.

Figure 4-7:
Open the workbook to the Start Here sheet.

	A	B	C	D	E	F
7						
8						
9						
10						
11						
12						

◀ ▶ │ Next Sheet │ Other Sheet │ **Start Here** │

How the macro works

This macro uses the workbook's Open event to start the workbook on the specified sheet when the workbook is opened:

```
Private Sub Workbook_Open()

'Step 1: Select the specified sheet
    Sheets("Start Here").Select

End Sub
```

The macro explicitly names the sheet the workbook should jump to when it's opened.

How to use the macro

To implement this macro, you need to copy and paste it into the Workbook_Open event code window. Placing the macro here allows it to run each time the workbook is opened:

1. **Activate Visual Basic Editor by pressing Alt+F11.**

2. **In the project window, find your project/workbook name and click the plus sign next to it to see all the sheets.**

3. **Click ThisWorkbook.**

4. **In the Event drop-down list (see Figure 4-8), select the Open event.**

5. **Type or paste the code in the newly created module, changing the sheet name, if necessary.**

Figure 4-8:
Enter your
code in the
Workbook
Open event.

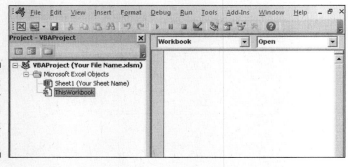

Opening a Specific Workbook Defined by the User

Want to give yourself or your users a quick way to search for and open a file? The next macro uses a simple technique that opens a friendly dialog box, allowing you to browse for and open the Excel file of your choosing.

How the macro works

This macro opens the dialog box you see in Figure 4-9, allowing the user to browse for and open an Excel file.

Figure 4-9: The Open dialog box activated by the macro.

Here's how this macro works:

```
Sub Macro1()

'Step 1: Define a String variable
    Dim FName As Variant
```

```
'Step 2: GetOpenFilename Method activates dialog box
    FName = Application.GetOpenFilename( _
            FileFilter:="Excel Workbooks,*.xl*", _
            Title:="Choose a Workbook to Open", _
            MultiSelect:=False)

'Step 3: If a file was chosen, open it!
    If FName <> False Then
    Workbooks.Open Filename:=FName
    End If

End Sub
```

In Step 1, the macro declares a Variant variable that holds the filename that the user chooses. FName is the name of your variable.

In Step 2, you use the GetOpenFilename method to call up a dialog box that allows you to browse and select the file you need.

The GetOpenFilename method supports a few customizable parameters. The FileFilter parameter allows you to specify the type of file you're looking for. The Title parameter allows you to change the title that appears at the top of the dialog box. The MultiSelect parameter allows you to limit the selection to one file.

If the user selects a file from the dialog box, the FName variable is filled with the chosen filename. In Step 3, you check for an empty FName variable. If the variable is not empty, you use the Open method of the Workbooks object to open the file.

How to use the macro

To implement this macro, you can copy and paste it into a standard module:

1. **Activate Visual Basic Editor by pressing Alt+F11 on your keyboard.**

2. **Right-click project/workbook name in the project window.**

3. **Choose Insert ⇨ Module.**

4. **Type or paste the code in the newly created module.**

5. **(Optional) Assign the macro to a button.**

   For details, see the section on assigning a macro to a button in Chapter 1.

Determining Whether a Workbook Is Already Open

The previous macro automatically opened a workbook based on the user's selection. As you think about automatically opening workbooks, consider what may happen if you attempt to open a book that is already open. In the non-VBA world, Excel attempts to open the file again, with the message shown in Figure 4-10 warning that any unsaved changes will be lost. You can protect against such an occurrence by checking whether a given file is already open before trying to open it again.

Figure 4-10:
Avoid this
warning
message.

How the macro works

The first thing to notice about this macro is that it is a function, not a Sub procedure. As you will see, making this macro a function enables you to pass any filename to it to test whether that file is already open.

The gist of this code is simple. You're testing a given filename to see if it can be assigned to an Object variable. Only opened workbooks can be assigned to an Object variable. When you try to assign a closed workbook to the variable, an error occurs.

If the given workbook can be assigned, the workbook is open; if an error occurs, the workbook is closed.

```
Function FileIsOpenTest(TargetWorkbook As String) As
          Boolean

'Step 1: Declare your variables
    Dim TestBook As Workbook

'Step 2: Tell Excel to resume on error
    On Error Resume Next

'Step 3: Try to assign the target workbook to TestBook
    Set TestBook = Workbooks(TargetWorkbook)
```

```
'Step 4: If no error occurred, workbook is already open
    If Err.Number = 0 Then
    FileIsOpenTest = True
    Else
    FileIsOpenTest = False
    End If

End Function
```

The first thing the macro does is to declare a String variable that will hold the filename that the user chooses. TestBook is the name of your String variable.

In Step 2, you tell Excel that there may be an error running this code an, in the event of an error, resume the code. Without this line, the code would simply stop when an error occurs. Again, you test a given filename to see if it can be assigned to an Object variable. If the given workbook can be assigned, it's open; if an error occurs, it's closed.

In Step 3, you attempt to assign the given workbook to the TestBook Object variable. The workbook you try to assign is a String variable called TargetWorkbook. TargetWorkbook is passed to the function in the function declarations (see the first line of the code). This structure eliminates the need to hard-code a workbook name, allowing you to pass it as a variable instead.

In Step 4, you simply check to see if an error occurred. If an error did not occur, the workbook is open, so you set the FileIsOpenTest to True. If an error occurred, the workbook is not open and you set the FileIsOpenTest to False.

Again, this function can be used to evaluate any file you pass to it, via its TargetWorkbook argument. This is the beauty of putting the macro into a function.

The following macro demonstrates how to implement this function. Here, you use the same macro you saw in the previous section, "Opening a Specific Workbook Defined by the User," but this time, you call the new FileIsOpenTest function to make sure that the user cannot open an already opened file:

```
Sub Macro1()
'Step 1: Define a String variable
    Dim FName As Variant
    Dim FNFileOnly As String
```

```
'Step 2: GetOpenFilename Method activates dialog box
    FName = Application.GetOpenFilename( _
            FileFilter:="Excel Workbooks,*.xl*", _
            Title:="Choose a Workbook to Open", _
            MultiSelect:=False)

'Step 3: Open the chosen file if not already opened
    If FName <> False Then
    FNFileOnly = StrReverse(Left(StrReverse(FName), _
                 InStr(StrReverse(FName), "\") - 1))

        If FileIsOpenTest(FNFileOnly) = True Then
            MsgBox "The given file is already open"
        Else
            Workbooks.Open Filename:=FName
        End If
    End If

End Sub
```

With this macro implemented, you get the friendlier message box shown in Figure 4-11.

Figure 4-11:
A cleaner, more concise message.

How to use the macro

To implement this macro, you can copy and paste both pieces of code into a standard module:

1. **Activate Visual Basic Editor by pressing Alt+F11.**

2. **Right-click the project/workbook name in the project window.**

3. **Choose Insert⇨Module.**

4. **Type or paste the code in the newly created module.**

5. **(Optional) Assign the macro to a button.**

   For details, see the section on assigning a macro to a button in Chapter 1.

Determining Whether a Workbook Exists in a Directory

You may have a process that manipulates a file somewhere on your PC. For example, you may need to open an existing workbook to add data to it on a daily basis. In this case, you may need to test to see whether the file you need to manipulate exists. The macro described in this section allows you to pass a file path to evaluate whether the file is there.

How the macro works

The first thing to notice about this macro is that it is a function, not a Sub procedure. Making this macro a function enables you to pass any file path to it.

In this macro, you use the Dir function, which returns a string that represents the name of the file that matches what you pass to it. This function can be used in lots of ways, but here, you use it to check whether the file path you pass to it exists:

```
Function FileExists(FPath As String) As Boolean

'Step 1: Declare your variables
    Dim FName As String

'Step 2: Use the Dir function to get the filename
    FName = Dir(FPath)

'Step 3:  If file exists, return True; else False
    If FName <> "" Then FileExists = True _
    Else: FileExists = False

End Function
```

Step 1 declares a String variable that holds the filename that returns from the Dir function. FName is the name of the String variable.

In Step 2, you attempt to set the FName variable. You do this by passing the FPath variable to the Dir function. This FPath variable is passed via the function declarations (see the first line of the code). This structure prevents you from having to hard-code a file path, passing it as a variable instead.

If the FName variable can't be set, the path you passed does not exist. Thus the FName variable is empty. Step 3 merely translates that result to a True or False expression.

Again, this function can be used to evaluate any file path you pass to it. This is the beauty of writing the macro as a function.

The following macro demonstrates how to use this function:

```
Sub Macro1()

    If FileExists("C:\Temp\MyNewBook.xlsx") = True Then
        MsgBox "File exists."
    Else
        MsgBox "File does not exist."
    End If

End Sub
```

How to use the macro

To implement this macro, you can copy and paste both pieces of code into a standard module:

1. **Activate Visual Basic Editor by pressing Alt+F11.**
2. **Right-click the project/workbook name in the project window.**
3. **Choose Insert ⇨ Module.**
4. **Type or paste the code in the newly created module.**

Closing All Workbooks at Once

One of the more annoying things in Excel is closing many workbooks at once. For each workbook you've opened, you need to activate the work, close it, and confirm the saving of changes. Excel has no easy way to close them all at once. This little macro takes care of that annoyance.

How the macro works

In this macro, the Workbooks collection loops through all opened workbooks. As the macro loops through each workbook, it saves and closes them down:

```
Sub Macro1()

'Step 1: Declare your variables
    Dim wb As Workbook
```

```
'Step 2: Loop through workbooks, save and close
    For Each wb In Workbooks
        wb.Close SaveChanges:=True
    Next wb

End Sub
```

Step 1 declares an Object variable that represents a Workbook object. This allows you to enumerate through all the open workbooks, capturing their names as you go.

Step 2 simply loops through the open workbooks, saving and closing them. If you don't want to save them, change the SaveChanges argument from True to False.

How to use the macro

The best place to store this macro is in your personal macro workbook. This way, the macro is always available to you. The personal macro workbook is loaded whenever you start Excel. In the VBE project window, it is named personal.xlsb.

1. **Activate Visual Basic Editor by pressing Alt+F11.**

2. **Right-click personal.xlb in the project window.**

3. **Choose Insert ⇨ Module.**

4. **Type or paste the code in the newly created module.**

If you don't see personal.xlb in your project window, it doesn't exist yet. You'll have record a macro using personal macro workbook as the destination.

To record the macro in your personal macro workbook, open the Record Macro dialog box. In the Store Macro In drop-down list, select Personal Macro Workbook. Then simply record a few cell clicks and stop recording. You can discard the recorded macro and replace it with this one.

Printing All Workbooks in a Directory

If you need to print from multiple workbooks in a directory, you can use the macro presented in this section.

How the macro works

In this macro, you use the Dir function to return a string that represents the name of the file that matches what you pass to it.

You use the Dir function to enumerate through all .xlsx files in a given directory, capturing each file's name. Then you open each file, print it, and then close it.

```
Sub Macro1()

'Step 1:Declare your variables
    Dim MyFiles As String

'Step 2: Specify a target directory
    MyFiles = Dir("C:\Temp\*.xlsx")
    Do While MyFiles <> ""

'Step 3: Open workbooks one by one
    Workbooks.Open "C:\Temp\" & MyFiles
    ActiveWorkbook.Sheets("Sheet1").PrintOut Copies:=1
    ActiveWorkbook.Close SaveChanges:=False

'Step 4: Next file in the directory
    MyFiles = Dir
    Loop

End Sub
```

Step 1 declares the MyFiles String variable that will capture each filename in the enumeration.

Step 2 uses the Dir function to specify the directory and file type you are looking for. Note that the code is looking for *.xlsx, so only xlsx files will be looped through. If you want to look for .xls files, you will need to specify that (along with the directory you need to search). The macro passes any filename it finds to the MyFiles String variable.

Step 3 opens the file and then prints one copy of Sheet1. Needless to say, you will probably want to change which sheets to print. You can also change the number of copies to print.

Step 4 loops back to find more files. If there are no more files, the MyFiles variable is blank and the loop and the macro end.

How to use the macro

To implement this macro, you can copy and paste it into a standard module:

1. **Activate Visual Basic Editor by pressing Alt+F11.**
2. **Right-click the project/workbook name in the project window.**
3. **Choose Insert ➪ Module.**
4. **Type or paste the code in the newly created module, modifying the print statement as needed.**

Preventing the Workbook from Closing Until a Cell Is Populated

There are times when you don't want a user closing out a workbook without entering a specific piece of data. In these situations, it would be useful to deny the user the ability to close the workbook until the target cell is filled in (see Figure 4-12). This is where the next macro comes in.

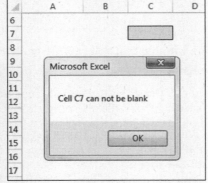

Figure 4-12:
Prevent
closing until
a specific
cell is
populated.

How the macro works

This code is triggered by the workbook's BeforeClose event. When you try to close the workbook, this event fires, running the code within. This macro checks to see if the target cell (cell C7, in this case) is empty. If it is empty, the close process is cancelled. If C7 is not empty, the workbook is saved and closed:

```
Private Sub Workbook_BeforeClose(Cancel As Boolean)

'Step 1: Check to see if cell C7 is blank
If Sheets("Sheet1").Range("C7").Value = "" Then

'Step 2: If cell is blank, cancel the close and tell user
    Cancel = True
    MsgBox "Cell C7 cannot be blank"

'Step 3: If cell is not blank, save and close
Else
    ActiveWorkbook.Close SaveChanges:=True
End If

End Sub
```

Step 1 checks to see whether C7 is blank.

If C7 is blank, Step 2 takes effect, cancelling the close process by passing True to the Cancel Boolean. Step 2 also activates a message box notifying the user of his or her stupidity (well, it's not quite that harsh, really).

In Step 3, if cell C7 is not blank, the workbook is saved and closed.

How to use the macro

To implement this macro, you need to copy and paste it into the Workbook_ BeforeClose event code window. Placing the macro here allows it to run each time you try to close the workbook:

1. **Activate Visual Basic Editor by pressing Alt+F11.**

2. **In the project window, find your project/workbook name and click the plus sign next to it to see all the sheets.**

3. **Click ThisWorkbook.**

4. **In the Event drop-down list (see Figure 4-13), select the BeforeClose event.**

5. **Type or paste the code in the newly created module.**

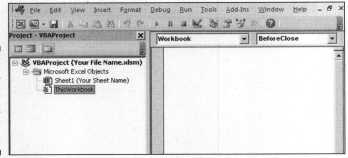

Figure 4-13:
Enter your
code in the
Workbook
BeforeClose
event.

Creating a Backup of a Current Workbook with Today's Date

You know that backing up your work is important. Now you can have a macro do it for you. This simple macro saves your workbook to a new file with today's date as part of the name.

How the macro works

The trick to this macro is piecing together the new filename as the path, today's date, and the original filename.

The path is captured by using the Path property of the ThisWorkbook object. Today's date is grabbed with the Date function.

By default, the Date function returns mm/dd/yyyy. Forward slashes would cause the file save to fail, so you format the date using hyphens instead (Format(Date, "mm-dd-yy")) because Windows does not allow forward slashes in filenames.

The last piece of the new filename is the original filename. You capture it by using the Name property of the ThisWorkbook object:

```
Sub Macro1()
'Step 1: Save workbook with new filename
    ThisWorkbook.SaveCopyAs _
    Filename:=ThisWorkbook.Path & "\" & _
    Format(Date, "mm-dd-yy") & " " & _
    ThisWorkbook.Name

End Sub
```

In the one and only step, the macro builds a new filename and uses the SaveCopyAs method to save the file.

How to use the macro

To implement this macro, you can copy and paste it into a standard module:

1. **Activate Visual Basic Editor by pressing Alt+F11.**
2. **Right-click the project/workbook name in the project window.**
3. **Choose Insert ⇨ Module.**
4. **Type or paste the code in the newly created module.**

Chapter 5

Working with Worksheets

Excel analysts can save time and gain efficiencies by using macros to automate tasks related to worksheets. Two common example tasks are unhiding all sheets in a workbook and printing all sheets at the same time. In this chapter, I cover some of the more useful macros related to worksheets.

Adding and Naming a New Worksheet

The chapter starts with one of the simplest worksheet-related automations you can apply with a macro: adding and naming a new worksheet.

How the macro works

When you read through the lines of the code, you'll see that this macro is relatively intuitive:

```
Sub Macro1()

'Step 1: Tell Excel what to do if error
    On Error GoTo MyError
```

```
'Step 2:  Add a sheet and name it
    Sheets.Add
    ActiveSheet.Name = _
    WorksheetFunction.Text(Now(), "m-d-yyyy h_mm_ss
         am/pm")
    Exit Sub


'Step 3: If here, an error happened; tell the user
    MyError:
    MsgBox "There is already a sheet called that."

End Sub
```

You must anticipate that if you give the new sheet a name that already exists, an error would occur. So in Step 1, the macro tells Excel to immediately skip to the line that says MyError (in Step 3) if there is an error.

Step 2 uses the Add method to add a new sheet. By default, the sheet is called Sheet*xx,* where *xx* represents the number of the sheet. You give the sheet a new name by changing the Name property of the ActiveSheet object. In this case, you're naming the worksheet with the current date and time.

As with workbooks, each time you use VBA to add a new sheet, the newly added sheet automatically becomes the active sheet. Finally, in Step 2, note that the macro exits the procedure. It has to do this so that it doesn't accidentally go into Step 3 (which comes into play only if an error occurs).

Step 3 notifies the user that the sheet name already exists. Again, this step should be activated only if an error occurs.

How to use the macro

To implement this macro, you can copy and paste it into a standard module:

1. **Activate Visual Basic Editor by pressing Alt+F11.**

2. **Right-click the project/workbook name in the project window.**

3. **Choose Insert ⇨ Module.**

4. **Type or paste the code in the newly created module.**

Deleting All but the Active Worksheet

At times, you may want to delete all but the active worksheet. In these situations, you can use this next macro.

How the macro works

The macro in this section loops through the worksheets, matching each worksheet name to the active sheet's name. Each time the macro loops, it deletes any unmatched worksheet. Note the use of the DisplayAlerts property in Step 4. This effectively turns off Excel's warnings so you don't have to confirm each delete.

```
Sub Macro1()

'Step 1:  Declare your variables
    Dim ws As Worksheet

'Step 2: Start looping through all worksheets
    For Each ws In ThisWorkbook.Worksheets

'Step 3: Check each worksheet name
    If ws.Name <> ThisWorkbook.ActiveSheet.Name Then

'Step 4: Turn off warnings and delete
    Application.DisplayAlerts = False
    ws.Delete
    Application.DisplayAlerts = True
    End If

'Step 5:  Loop to next worksheet
    Next ws

End Sub
```

The macro first declares an object called ws. This step creates a memory container for each worksheet it loops through.

In Step 2, the macro begins to loop, telling Excel it will evaluate all worksheets in this workbook. There is a difference between ThisWorkbook and ActiveWorkbook. The ThisWorkBook object refers to the workbook that contains the code. The ActiveWorkBook object refers to the currently active workbook. They often return the same object, but if the workbook running the code is not the active workbook, they return different objects. In this case, you don't want to risk deleting sheets in other workbooks, so you use ThisWorkBook.

In Step 3, the macro simply compares the active sheet name to the sheet that is currently being looped.

In Step 4, if the sheet names are different, the macro deletes the sheet. As mentioned, you use DisplayAlerts to suppress any confirmation checks from Excel. If you want to be warned before deleting the sheets, you can omit Application. DisplayAlerts = False. Omitting the DisplayAlerts statement will ensure that you get the message in Figure 5-1, allowing you to back out of the decision to delete worksheets.

In Step 5, the macro loops back to get the next sheet. After all the sheets are evaluated, the macro ends.

Figure 5-1: Omit the Display-Alerts statement to see warning messages.

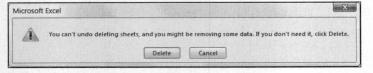

How to use the macro

To implement this macro, you can copy and paste it into a standard module:

1. **Activate Visual Basic Editor by pressing Alt+F11.**

2. **Right-click the project/workbook name in the project window.**

3. **Choose Insert ⇨ Module.**

4. **Type or paste the code in the newly created module.**

When you use ThisWorkbook instead of ActiveWorkbook in a macro, you can't run the macro from the personal macro workbook. Why? Because ThisWorkbook would refer to the personal macro workbook, not to the workbook to which the macro should apply.

Hiding All but the Active Worksheet

You may not want to delete all but the active sheet as you did in the preceding macro. Instead, a more gentle option is to simply hide the sheets. Excel doesn't let you hide all sheets in a workbook; at least one has to be displayed. However, you can hide all but the active sheet.

How the macro works

The macro in this section loops through the worksheets and matches each worksheet name to the active sheet's name. Each time the macro loops, it hides any unmatched worksheet.

```
Sub Macro1()

'Step 1:  Declare your variables
    Dim ws As Worksheet

'Step 2: Start looping through all worksheets
    For Each ws In ThisWorkbook.Worksheets

'Step 3: Check each worksheet name
    If ws.Name <> ThisWorkbook.ActiveSheet.Name Then

'Step 4: Hide the sheet
    ws.Visible = xlSheetHidden
    End If

'Step 5:  Loop to next worksheet
    Next ws

End Sub
```

Step 1 declares an object called ws. This step creates a memory container for each worksheet that the macro loops through.

Step 2 begins the looping, telling Excel to evaluate all worksheets in this workbook. Note the difference between ThisWorkbook and ActiveWorkbook. The ThisWorkBook object refers to the workbook that contains the code. The ActiveWorkBook object refers to the currently active workbook. They often return the same object, but if the workbook running the code is not the active workbook, they return different objects. In this case, you don't want to risk hiding sheets in other workbooks, so you use ThisWorkBook.

In Step 3, the macro simply compares the active sheet name to the sheet that is currently being looped.

If the sheet names are different, the macro hides the sheet in Step 4.

In Step 5, you loop back to get the next sheet. After all sheets are evaluated, the macro ends.

Note that you use xlsheetHidden in your macro. This property applies the default hide state you would normally get when you right-click a sheet and select Hide. In this default hide state, a user can right-click any tab and choose Unhide, which displays all hidden sheets. But another hide state is more clandestine than the default. If you use xlSheetVeryHidden to hide your sheets, users will not be able to see them at all — even if they right-click a tab and choose Unhide. The only way to unhide a sheet hidden in this manner is to use VBA.

How to use the macro

To implement this macro, you can copy and paste it into a standard module:

1. **Activate Visual Basic Editor by pressing Alt+F11.**
2. **Right-click the project/workbook name in the project window.**
3. **Choose Insert⇨Module.**
4. **Type or paste the code in the newly created module.**

Unhiding All Worksheets in a Workbook

If you've ever had to unhide multiple sheets in Excel, you know what a pain it is. You are forced to use the Unhide dialog box shown in Figure 5-2 to unhide one sheet at a time.

Figure 5-2:
Without a macro, you're stuck using the Unhide dialog box to unhide one worksheet at a time.

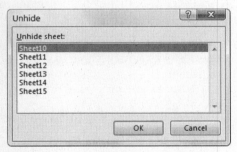

Although that may not sound like a big deal, it gets to be a pain fast when you have to unhide 10 or more sheets. The macro in this section makes easy work of the task.

How the macro works

This macro loops through the worksheets and changes their visible state.

```
Sub Macro1()

'Step 1:  Declare your variables
    Dim ws As Worksheet

'Step 2: Start looping through all worksheets
    For Each ws In ActiveWorkbook.Worksheets

'Step 3:  Loop to next worksheet
    ws.Visible = xlSheetVisible
    Next ws

End Sub
```

Step 1 declares an object called ws. This step creates a memory container for each worksheet that the macro loops through.

In Step 2, the macro starts the looping, telling Excel to enumerate through all worksheets in this workbook.

Step 3 changes the visible state to xlSheetVisible. Then it loops back to get the next worksheet.

How to use the macro

The best place to store this macro is in your personal macro workbook. That way, the macro is always available to you. The personal macro workbook is loaded whenever you start Excel. In the VBE project window, it is named personal.xlsb.

1. **Activate Visual Basic Editor by pressing Alt+F11.**

2. **Right-click personal.xlb in the project window.**

3. **Choose Insert ⇨ Module.**

4. **Type or paste the code in the newly created module.**

If you don't see personal.xlb in your project window, the file doesn't exist yet. You'll have to record a macro using personal macro workbook as the destination.

To record the macro in your personal macro workbook, display the Record Macro dialog box before you start recording. Then click the Store Macro In drop-down box and select the Personal Macro Workbook option. Simply record a few cell clicks and then stop recording. You can discard the recorded macro and replace it with this one.

Moving Worksheets Around

We've all had to rearrange a spreadsheet so that some sheets come before or after other sheets. If you find that you have to do this often, the macro in this section can help.

How the macro works

When you want to rearrange sheets, you use the Move method of either the Sheets object or the ActiveSheet object. When using the Move method, you specify where to move the sheet to by using the After argument, the Before argument, or both.

```
Sub Macro1()

'Move the active sheet to the end
    ActiveSheet.Move After:=Worksheets(Worksheets.Count)

'Move the active sheet to the beginning
    ActiveSheet.Move Before:=Worksheets(1)

'Move Sheet 1 before Sheet 12
    Sheets("Sheet1").Move Before:=Sheets("Sheet12")

End Sub
```

This macro demonstrates how to move the active worksheet to three locations:

✔ **Move the active sheet to the end:** When you need to move a worksheet to the end of the workbook, you essentially want to tell Excel to move the sheet after the last sheet. But there's no code in VBA that lets you point to the last sheet. However, you *can* find the maximum count of worksheets, and use that number as an index for the Worksheets object. For example, you could enter Worksheets(1) to point to the first sheet in a workbook, and enter Worksheet(3) to point to the third sheet in the workbook. To point to the last sheet in the workbook, you could replace the index number with the Worksheets.Count property. Worksheets.Count will give you the total number of worksheets, which will always be the same number as the index for the last sheet. Thus Worksheet(Worksheets.Count) will point to the last sheet.

✔ **Move the active sheet to the beginning:** Moving a sheet to the beginning of the workbook is simple. Use Worksheets(1) to point to the first sheet in the workbook, and then move the active sheet before that one.

✔ **Move Sheet 1 before Sheet X:** You can also move a sheet before or after another sheet simply by calling that other sheet out by name. In the example demonstrated in the preceding macro, you are moving Sheet1 before Sheet12.

How to use the macro

The best place to store this kind of a macro is in your personal macro workbook so that the macro is always available to you. The personal macro workbook is loaded whenever you start Excel. In the VBE project window, it is named personal.xlsb.

1. **Activate Visual Basic Editor by pressing Alt+F11.**

2. **Right-click personal.xlb in the project window.**

3. **Choose Insert⇨Module.**

4. **Type or paste the code in the newly created module.**

If you don't see personal.xlb in your project window, the file doesn't exist yet. You'll have to record a macro, using personal macro workbook as the destination.

To record the macro in your personal macro workbook, display the Record Macro dialog box before you start recording. Then click the Store Macro In drop-down box and select the Personal Macro Workbook option. Simply record a few cell clicks and then stop recording. You can discard the recorded macro and replace it with this one.

Sorting Worksheets by Name

You may often need to sort worksheets alphabetically by name (see Figure 5-3). You would think Excel would have a native function to do this, but alas, it does not. If you don't want to manually sort your spreadsheets, use this macro to do it for you.

Figure 5-3:
Sort your
worksheets
in alphabeti-
cal order.

How the macro works

The macro in this section looks more complicated than it is. The macro simply iterates through the sheets in the workbook, comparing the current sheet to the previous one. If the name of previous sheet is greater than the current sheet (alphabetically), the macro moves the current sheet before it. By the time all the iterations are completed, you have a sorted workbook!

```
Sub Macro1()

'Step 1: Declare your variables
    Dim CurrentSheetIndex As Integer
    Dim PrevSheetIndex As Integer

'Step 2: Set the starting counts and start looping
    For CurrentSheetIndex = 1 To Sheets.Count
    For PrevSheetIndex = 1 To CurrentSheetIndex - 1

'Step 3: Check current sheet against previous sheet
    If UCase(Sheets(PrevSheetIndex).Name) > _
       UCase(Sheets(CurrentSheetIndex).Name) Then

'Step 4: Move if current sheet comes before previous sheet
    Sheets(CurrentSheetIndex).Move _
    Before:=Sheets(PrevSheetIndex)
    End If

'Step 5 Loop back to iterate again
    Next PrevSheetIndex
    Next CurrentSheetIndex

End Sub
```

Note that this technique performs text-based sorting, so you may not get the results you were expecting when working with number-based sheet names. For instance, Sheet10 will come before Sheet2 because textually, 1 comes before 2. Excel can't do number-based sorting (in which 2 would come before 10).

Step 1 declares two integer variables. The CurrentSheetIndex variable holds the index number for the current sheet iteration, and the PrevSheetIndex variable holds the index number for the previous sheet iteration.

In Step 2, the macro starts iteration counts for both variables. Note that the count for PrevSheetIndex is one number behind CurrentSheetIndex. After the counts are set, you start looping.

In Step 3, you check to see whether the name of the previous sheet is greater than that of the current sheet. Note the UCase function, which you use to get both names in the same uppercase state. This function prevents sorting errors due to different case states.

Step 4 is reached only if the previous sheet name is greater than the current sheet name. In this step, you use the Move method to move the current sheet before the previous sheet.

In Step 5, you go back around to the start of the loop. Every iteration of the loop increments both variables up one number until the last worksheet is touched. After all iterations have completed, the macro ends.

How to use the macro

The best place to store this macro is in your personal macro workbook so that the macro is always available to you. The personal macro workbook is loaded whenever you start Excel. In the VBE project window, it is named personal.xlsb.

1. **Activate Visual Basic Editor by pressing Alt+F11.**
2. **Right-click personal.xlb in the project window.**
3. **Choose Insert ⇨ Module.**
4. **Type or paste the code in the newly created module.**

If you don't see personal.xlb in your project window, the file doesn't exist yet. You'll have to record a macro, using personal macro workbook as the destination.

To record the macro in your personal macro workbook, display the Record Macro dialog box before you start recording. Then click the Store Macro

In drop-down box and select the Personal Macro Workbook option. Simply record a few cell clicks and then stop recording. You can discard the recorded macro and replace it with this one.

Grouping Worksheets by Color

Many of us assign colors to our worksheet tabs. You can right-click any tab and select the Tab Color option (shown in Figure 5-4) to choose a color for your tab.

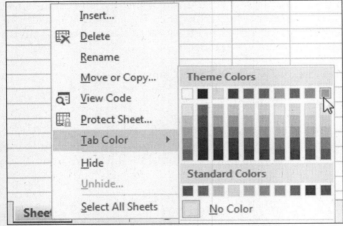

Figure 5-4:
Choose a
tab color for
the sheet.

This technique allows for the visual confirmation that data in one tab is related to data in another tab because both tabs are the same color. When you have many colored sheets, it's often useful to group tabs with the same color for ease of navigation.

The macro in this section groups worksheets based on their tab colors.

How the macro works

You may think it's impossible to sort or group by color, but Excel offers a way. Excel assigns an index number to every color. A light yellow color may have an index number of 36, whereas a maroon color has the index number 42.

This macro iterates through the sheets in the workbook, comparing the tab color index of the current sheet to that of the previous one. If the previous sheet has the same color index number as the current sheet, the macro moves the current sheet before it. By the time all the iterations are completed, all sheets are grouped based on their tab color.

```
Sub Macro1()

'Step 1: Declare your variables
    Dim CurrentSheetIndex As Integer
    Dim PrevSheetIndex As Integer

'Step 2: Set the starting counts and start looping
    For CurrentSheetIndex = 1 To Sheets.Count
    For PrevSheetIndex = 1 To CurrentSheetIndex - 1

'Step 3: Check current sheet against previous sheet
    If Sheets(PrevSheetIndex).Tab.ColorIndex = _
    Sheets(CurrentSheetIndex).Tab.ColorIndex Then


'Step 4: Move if current and previous color indexes match
        Sheets(PrevSheetIndex).Move _
    Before:=Sheets(CurrentSheetIndex)
    End If

'Step 5 Loop back to iterate again
    Next PrevSheetIndex
    Next CurrentSheetIndex

End Sub
```

Step 1 declares two integer variables. The CurrentSheetIndex variable holds the index number for the current sheet iteration, and the PrevSheetIndex variable holds the index number for the previous sheet iteration.

Step 2 starts iteration counts for both variables. Note that the count for PrevSheetIndex is one number behind CurrentSheetIndex. After the counts are set, the macro starts looping.

In Step 3, the macro checks to see whether the color index of the previous sheet is the same as that of the current sheet. Note the use of the Tab.ColorIndex property.

Step 4 is reached only if the color index of the previous sheet is equal to the color index of the current sheet. In this step, the macro uses the Move method to move the current sheet before the previous sheet.

In Step 5, the macro goes back to the start of the loop. Every iteration of the loop increments both variables up one number until the last worksheet is touched. After all of the iterations have run, the macro ends.

How to use the macro

The best place to store this macro is in your personal macro workbook so that the macro is always available to you. The personal macro workbook is loaded whenever you start Excel. In the VBE project window, it is named personal.xlsb.

1. **Activate Visual Basic Editor by pressing Alt+F11.**
2. **Right-click personal.xlb in the project window.**
3. **Choose Insert ⇨ Module.**
4. **Type or paste the code in the newly created module.**

If you don't see personal.xlb in your project window, the file doesn't exist yet. You'll have to record a macro, using personal macro workbook as the destination.

To record the macro in your personal macro workbook, display the Record Macro dialog box before you start recording. Then click the Store Macro In drop-down box and select the Personal Macro Workbook option. Simply record a few cell clicks and then stop recording. You can discard the recorded macro and replace it with this one.

Copying a Worksheet to a New Workbook

In Excel, you can manually copy an entire sheet to a new workbook by right-clicking the target sheet and selecting the Move or Copy option. Unfortunately, if you try to record a macro while you do this, the macro recorder fails to accurately write the code to reflect the task. When you need to programmatically copy an entire sheet to a new workbook, the macro in this section delivers.

How the macro works

In this macro, the active sheet is first copied. Then you use the Before parameter to send the copy to a new workbook that is created on the fly. The copied sheet is positioned as the first sheet in the new workbook.

The use of the ThisWorkbook object is important here. It ensures that the active sheet that is being copied is from the workbook that contains the code, not from the newly created workbook.

```
Sub Macro1()

'Copy sheet, and send to new workbook
    ThisWorkbook.ActiveSheet.Copy _
    Before:=Workbooks.Add.Worksheets(1)

End Sub
```

How to use the macro

To implement this macro, you can copy and paste it into a standard module:

1. **Activate Visual Basic Editor by pressing Alt+F11.**
2. **Right-click the project/workbook name in the project window.**
3. **Choose Insert ⇨ Module.**
4. **Type or paste the code in the newly created module.**

Creating a Workbook for Each Worksheet

Many Excel analysts need to parse their workbooks into separate books per worksheet tab. In other words, they need to create a new workbook for each worksheet in their existing workbook. You can imagine what an ordeal this task would be if you had to do it manually. The following macro helps automate this task.

How the macro works

In this macro, you are looping through the worksheets, copying each sheet, and then sending the copy to a new workbook that is created on the fly. The thing to note here is that the newly created workbooks are saved in the same directory as your original workbook, with the same filename as the copied sheet (wb.SaveAs ThisWorkbook.Path & "\" & ws.Name).

```
Sub Macro1()

'Step 1:  Declare your variables
    Dim ws As Worksheet
    Dim wb As Workbook
```

```
'Step 2:  Start looping through sheets
    For Each ws In ThisWorkbook.Worksheets

'Step 3:  Create new workbook and save it
    Set wb = Workbooks.Add
    wb.SaveAs ThisWorkbook.Path & "\" & ws.Name

'Step 4:  Copy the target sheet to the new workbook
    ws.Copy Before:=wb.Worksheets(1)
    wb.Close SaveChanges:=True

'Step 5:  Loop back to the next worksheet
    Next ws

End Sub
```

Not all valid worksheet names translate to valid filenames.

Windows has specific rules regarding filenames. You can't use these characters when naming a file: backslash (\), forward slash (/), colon (:), asterisk (*), question mark (?), pipe (|), double quote ("), greater than (>) and less than (<).

The twist is that you can use a few of these restricted characters in your sheet names; specifically, double quote, pipe, greater than, and less than. So, as you run this macro, naming the newly created files to match the sheet name may cause an error. For instance, the macro will throw an error if you try to create a new file from a sheet called May|Revenue (because of the pipe character).

Step 1 declares two object variables. The ws variable creates a memory container for each worksheet through which the macro loops. The wb variable creates the container for the new workbooks you create.

In Step 2, the macro starts looping through the sheets. The use of the ThisWorkbook object ensures that the active sheet that is being copied is from the workbook containing the code, not from the new workbook that is created.

In Step 3, you create the new workbook and save it. You save this new book in the same path as the original workbook (ThisWorkbook). The filename is set to the same name as the currently active sheet.

Step 4 copies the currently active sheet and uses the Before parameter to send it to the new book as the first tab.

Step 5 loops back to get the next sheet. After all sheets have been evaluated, the macro ends.

This macro will not work on a workbook that has not been initially saved — that is to say, saved at least one time.

How to use the macro

To implement this macro, you can copy and paste it into a standard module:

1. **Activate Visual Basic Editor by pressing Alt+F11.**
2. **Right-click the project/workbook name in the project window.**
3. **Choose Insert ⇨ Module.**
4. **Type or paste the code in the newly created module.**

Printing Specified Worksheets

If you want to print specific sheets manually in Excel, you need to hold down the Ctrl key, select the sheets you want to print, and then click Print. If you do this often enough, you may want to consider using the simple macro in this section.

How the macro works

This macro is easy. All you have to do is pass in an array the sheets you want printed, and then you use the PrintOut method to trigger the print job. All the sheets you have entered are printed in one go.

```
Sub Macro1()

'Print certain sheets
    ActiveWorkbook.Sheets( _
    Array("Sheet1", "Sheet3", "Sheet5")).PrintOut
        Copies:=1

End Sub
```

Want to print all worksheets in a workbook? The following macro is even easier:

```
Sub Macro1()

'Print all sheets
    ActiveWorkbook.Worksheets.PrintOut Copies:=1

End Sub
```

How to use the macro

The best place to store this macro is in your personal macro workbook so that the macro is always available to you. The personal macro workbook is loaded whenever you start Excel. In the VBE project window, it is named personal.xlsb.

1. **Activate Visual Basic Editor by pressing Alt+F11.**

2. **Right-click personal.xlb in the project window.**

3. **Choose Insert ⇨ Module.**

4. **Type or paste the code in the newly created module.**

If you don't see personal.xlb in your project window, the file doesn't exist yet. You'll have to record a macro using Personal Macro Workbook as the destination.

To record the macro in your personal macro workbook, display the Record Macro dialog box before you start recording. Then click the Store Macro In drop-down box and select the Personal Macro Workbook option t. Simply record a couple of cell clicks and then stop recording. You can discard the recorded macro and replace it with this one.

Protecting All Worksheets

Before you distribute your workbook, you may want to apply sheet protection to all the sheets. However, as you can see in Figure 5-5, Excel will disable the Protect Sheet command if you try to protect multiple sheets at one time. You will be forced to protect one sheet at a time.

Figure 5-5:
The Protect
Sheet
command
is disabled
if you try
to protect
more than
one sheet at
a time.

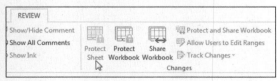

You can use the macro in this section to protect all sheets at one time.

How the macro works

In this macro, you loop through the worksheets and simply apply protection with a password. The Password argument defines the password needed to remove the protection. The Password argument is optional. If you omit it, the sheet will still be protected; you just won't need to enter a password to unprotect it.

Excel passwords are case-sensitive, so you'll want pay attention to the exact capitalization you are using in your macro.

```
Sub Macro1()

'Step 1:  Declare your variables
    Dim ws As Worksheet

'Step 2: Start looping through all worksheets
    For Each ws In ActiveWorkbook.Worksheets

'Step 3:  Protect and loop to next worksheet
    ws.Protect Password:="RED"
    Next ws

End Sub
```

Step 1 declares an object called ws. This step creates a memory container for each worksheet you loop through.

Step 2 starts the looping, telling Excel that you want to enumerate through all worksheets in this workbook.

In Step 3, the macro applies protection with the given password, and then loops back to get the worksheet.

How to use the macro

The best place to store this macro is in your personal macro workbook so that the macro is always available to you. The personal macro workbook is loaded whenever you start Excel. In the VBE project window, it is named personal.xlsb.

1. **Activate Visual Basic Editor by pressing Alt+F11.**

2. **Right-click personal.xlb in the project window.**

3. **Choose Insert ⇨ Module.**

4. **Type or paste the code in the newly created module.**

If you don't see personal.xlb in your project window, the file doesn't exist yet. You'll have to record a macro using Personal Macro Workbook as the destination.

To record the macro in your personal macro workbook, display the Record Macro dialog box before you start recording. Then click the Store Macro In drop-down box and select the Personal Macro Workbook option. Then simply record a few cell clicks and then stop recording. You can discard the recorded macro and replace it with this one.

Unprotecting All Worksheets

You may find yourself constantly having to unprotect multiple worksheets manually. However, as you can see in Figure 5-6, Excel will disable the Unprotect Sheet command if you try to unprotect multiple sheets at one time. You'll be forced to unprotect one sheet at a time.

Figure 5-6:
The Unprotect Sheet command is disabled if you try to unprotect more than one sheet at a time.

You can use the macro in this section to unprotect all sheets automatically.

How the macro works

The macro loops through the worksheets and uses the Password argument to unprotect each sheet:

```
Sub Macro1()

'Step 1:  Declare your variables
    Dim ws As Worksheet
```

```
'Step 2: Start looping through all worksheets
    For Each ws In ActiveWorkbook.Worksheets
'Step 3:  Loop to next worksheet
    ws.UnProtect Password:="RED"
    Next ws

End Sub
```

Step 1 declares an object called ws. This step creates a memory container for each worksheet you loop through.

Step 2 starts the looping, telling Excel to enumerate through all worksheets in this workbook.

Step 3 unprotects the active sheet, providing the password as needed, and then loops back to get the worksheet.

The assumption is that all worksheets that need to be unprotected have the same password. If this not the case, you need to explicitly unprotect each sheet with its corresponding password:

```
Sub Macro1()

Sheets("Sheet1").UnProtect Password:="RED"
Sheets("Sheet2").UnProtect Password:="BLUE"
Sheets("Sheet3").UnProtect Password:="YELLOW"
Sheets("Sheet4").UnProtect Password:="GREEN"

End Sub
```

How to use the macro

The best place to store this kind of a macro is in your personal macro workbook so that the macro is always available to you. The personal macro workbook is loaded whenever you start Excel. In the VBE project window, it will be named personal.xlsb.

1. **Activate Visual Basic Editor by pressing Alt+F11.**

2. **Right-click personal.xlb in the project window.**

3. **Choose Insert ⇨ Module.**

4. **Type or paste the code in the newly created module.**

If you don't see personal.xlb in your project window, the file doesn't exist yet. You'll have to record a macro, using Personal Macro Workbook as the destination.

To record the macro in your personal macro workbook, display the Record Macro dialog box before you start recording. Then click the Store Macro In drop-down box and select the Personal Macro Workbook option. Simply record a few cell clicks and then stop recording. You can discard the recorded macro and replace it with this one.

Creating a Table of Contents for Your Worksheets

With the exception of sorting worksheets, creating a table of contents for the worksheets in a workbook is the most commonly requested Excel macro. The reason is probably not lost on you because you often work with files that have more worksheet tabs than can easily be seen or navigated. A table of contents like the one in Figure 5-7 helps.

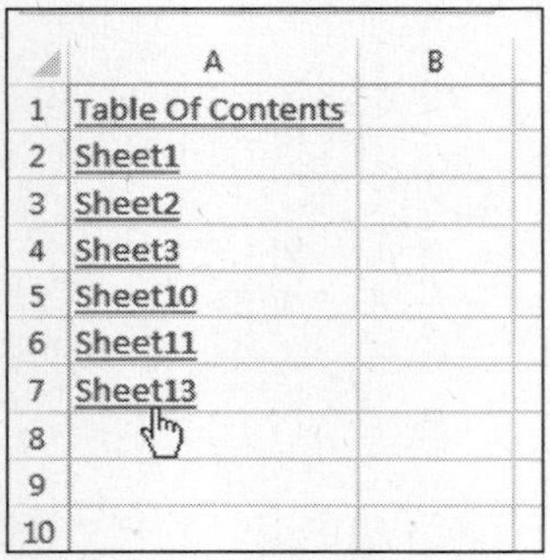

Figure 5-7:
A table of contents can help you more easily navigate your workbook.

	A	B
1	Table Of Contents	
2	Sheet1	
3	Sheet2	
4	Sheet3	
5	Sheet10	
6	Sheet11	
7	Sheet13	
8		
9		
10		

The following macro not only creates a list of worksheet names in the workbook but also ads hyperlinks so that you can easily jump to a sheet with a simple click.

How the macro works

It's easy to get intimidated when looking at the macro in this section because a lot is going on. However, if you step back and consider the few simple actions it does, it becomes less scary. The macro

- Removes any previous Table of Contents sheet
- Creates a new Table of Contents sheet

✔ Grabs the name of each worksheet and pastes it to the table of contents

✔ Adds a hyperlink to each entry in the table of contents

That doesn't sound so bad. Now look at the code:

```
Sub Macro1()

'Step 1: Declare your variables
    Dim i As Long

'Step 2:  Delete previous TOC if it exists
    On Error Resume Next
    Application.DisplayAlerts = False
    Sheets("Table Of Contents").Delete
    Application.DisplayAlerts = True
    On Error GoTo 0

'Step 3:  Add a new TOC sheet as the first sheet
    ThisWorkbook.Sheets.Add _
    Before:=ThisWorkbook.Worksheets(1)
    ActiveSheet.Name = "Table Of Contents"

'Step 4: Start the i counter
    For i = 1 To Sheets.Count

'Step 5: Select next available row
    ActiveSheet.Cells(i, 1).Select

'Step 6:  Add sheet name and hyperlink
    ActiveSheet.Hyperlinks.Add _
    Anchor:=ActiveSheet.Cells(i, 1), _
    Address:="", _
    SubAddress:="'" & Sheets(i).Name & "'!A1", _
    TextToDisplay:=Sheets(i).Name

'Step 7: Loop back and increment i
    Next i

End Sub
```

Step 1 declares an Integer variable called i to serve as the counter as the macro iterates through the sheets.

Note that this macro is not looping through the sheets the way previous macros in this chapter did. In previous macros, you looped through the Worksheets collection and selected each worksheet there. In this procedure, you use a counter (your i variable). The main reason is because you have to not only keep track of the sheets but also enter each sheet name on a new row in a table of contents. The idea is that as the counter progresses through the sheets, it also serves to move the cursor down in the table of contents so each new entry goes on a new row.

Step 2 essentially attempts to delete any previous sheet called Table of Contents. Because there may not be any Table of Contents sheet to delete, you have to start Step 2 with the On Error Resume Next error handler. This handler tells Excel to continue the macro if an error is encountered here. You then delete the Table of Contents sheet using the DisplayAlerts method, which effectively turns off Excel's warnings so you don't have to confirm the deletion. Finally, you reset the error handler to trap all errors again by entering On Error GoTo 0.

In Step 3, you add a new sheet to the workbook by using the Before argument to position the new sheet as the first sheet. You then name the sheet Table of Contents. As mentioned, when you add a new worksheet, it automatically becomes the active sheet. Because this new sheet has the focus throughout the procedure, any references to ActiveSheet in this code refer to the Table of Contents sheet.

Step 4 starts the i counter at 1 and ends it at the maximum count of all sheets in the workbook. Again, instead of looping through the Worksheets collection like you did in previous macros, you simply use the i counter as an index number that you can pass to the Sheets object. When the maximum number is reached, the macro ends.

Step 5 selects the corresponding row in the Table of Contents sheet. That is to say, if the i counter is on 1, it selects the first row in the Table of Contents sheet. If the i counter is at 2, it selects the second row, and so on.

You select rows by using the Cells item, which provides a handy way of selecting ranges through code. It requires only relative row and column positions as parameters. So Cells(1,1) translates to row 1, column 1 (or cell A1). Cells(5, 3) translates to row 5, column 3 (or cell C5). The numeric parameters in the Cells item are particularly useful when you want to loop through a series of rows or columns by using an incrementing index number.

Step 6 uses the Hyperlinks.Add method to add the sheet name and hyperlinks to the selected cell. This step feeds the Hyperlinks.Add method the parameters it needs to build out the hyperlinks.

The last step in the macro loops back to increment the i counter to the next count. When the i counter reaches a number that equals the count of worksheets in the workbook, the macro ends.

How to use the macro

To implement this macro, you can copy and paste it into a standard module:

1. **Activate Visual Basic Editor by pressing Alt+F11.**
2. **Right-click project/workbook name in the project window.**
3. **Choose Insert ⇨ Module.**
4. **Type or paste the code in the newly created module.**

Zooming In and Out of a Worksheet with Double-Click

Some spreadsheets are huge and you're forced to shrink the font size down so that you can see a decent portion of the spreadsheet on the screen. If you find that you are constantly zooming in and out of a spreadsheet, alternating between scanning large sections of data and reading specific cells, use the handy macro in this section, which will auto-zoom on a double-click.

How the macro works

With this macro in place, you can double-click a cell in the spreadsheet to zoom in 200 percent. Double-click again and Excel zooms back to 100 percent. You can change the values and complexity in the code to fit your needs.

```
Private Sub Worksheet_BeforeDoubleClick(ByVal Target As
          Range, Cancel As Boolean)

'Check current zoom state
'Zoom to 100% if at 100
'Zoom 200% if currently at 100
    If ActiveWindow.Zoom <> 100 Then
    ActiveWindow.Zoom = 100
    Else
    ActiveWindow.Zoom = 200
    End If

End Sub
```

The side effect of double-clicking a cell is that it goes into edit mode. You can exit edit mode by pressing the escape key (Esc). If you find it annoying to keep pressing Esc when triggering this macro, add the following statement to the end of the procedure:

```
Application.SendKeys ("{ESC}")
```

This statement mimics an Esc keypress.

How to use the macro

To implement this macro, you need to copy and paste it into the Worksheet_ BeforeDoubleClick event code window. Placing the macro there allows it to run each time you double-click the sheet.

1. **Activate Visual Basic Editor by pressing Alt+F11.**

2. **In the project window, find your project/workbook name and click the plus sign next to it to see all the sheets.**

3. **Click the sheet from which you want to trigger the code.**

4. **In the Event drop-down list, select the BeforeDoubleClick event (see Figure 5-8).**

5. **Type or paste the code in the newly created module.**

Figure 5-8:
Enter your
code in the
Worksheet
Before
DoubleClick
event.

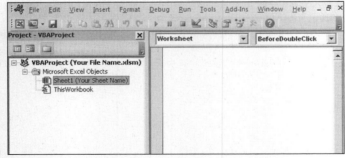

Highlighting the Active Row and Column

When looking at a table of numbers, it would be nice if Excel could automatically highlight the row and column you're on (as demonstrated in Figure 5-9). This effect gives your eyes a lead line up and down the column as well as left and right across the row.

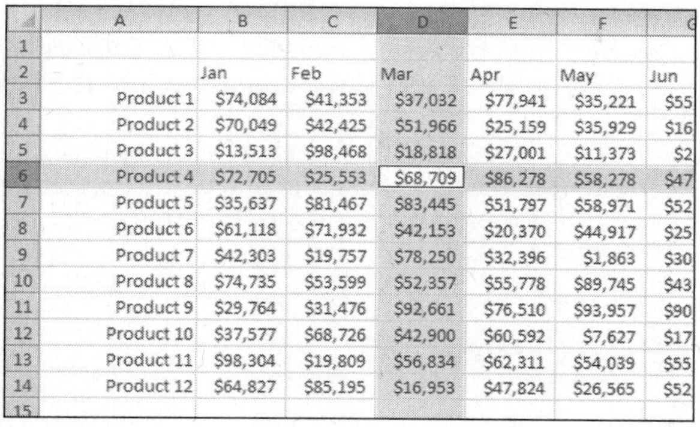

Figure 5-9:
The high-
lighted row
and column
make it easy
to track
data hori-
zontally and
vertically.

The following macro enables the effect you see in Figure 5-9 with just a simple double-click. When the macro is in place, Excel highlights the row and column for the active cell, greatly improving your ability to view and edit a large grid.

How the macro works

Take a look at how this macro works:

```
Private Sub Worksheet_BeforeDoubleClick(ByVal Target As
        Range, Cancel As Boolean)

'Step 1:  Declare your variables
    Dim strRange As String

'Step 2:  Build the range string
    strRange = Target.Cells.Address & "," & _
            Target.Cells.EntireColumn.Address & "," & _
            Target.Cells.EntireRow.Address

'Step 3: Pass the range string to a range
    Range(strRange).Select

End Sub
```

In Step 1, you first declare an object called strRange. This step creates a memory container you can use to build a range string.

A *range string* is nothing more than the address for a range. "A1" is a range string that points to cell A1. "A1:G5" is also a range string; it points to a range of cells encompassing cells A1 to G5. In Step 2, you're building a range string that encompasses the double-clicked cell (called Target in this macro), the entire active row, and the entire active column. The Address property for these three ranges is captured and pieced together into the strRange variable.

In Step 3, you feed the strRange variable as the address for a Range.Select statement. This line of the code finally highlights the double-clicked selection.

How to use the macro

To implement this macro, you need to copy and paste it into the Worksheet_ BeforeDoubleClick event code window. Placing the macro there allows it to run each time you double-click on the sheet.

1. **Activate Visual Basic Editor by pressing Alt+F11.**

2. **In the project window, find your project/workbook name and click the plus sign next to it to see all the sheets.**

3. **Click the sheet from which you want to trigger the code.**

4. **In the Event drop-down list, select the BeforeDoubleClick event (see Figure 5-10).**

5. **Type or paste the code in the newly created module.**

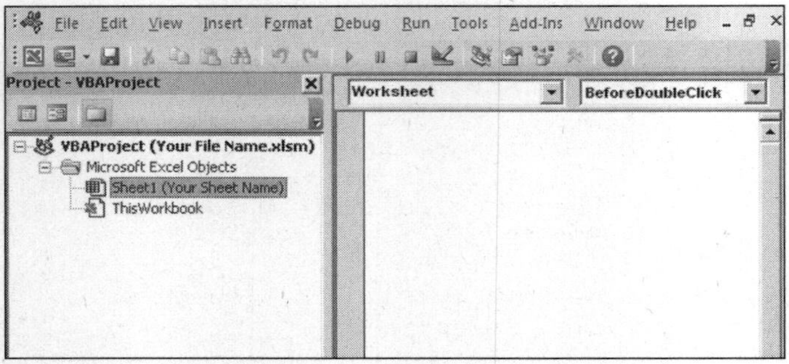

Figure 5-10:
Enter your code in the Worksheet Before DoubleClick event.

Part III
One-Touch Data Manipulation

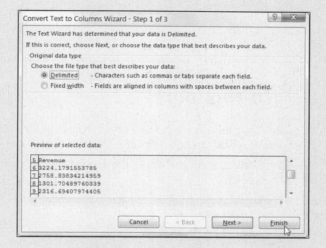

In this part . . .

- ✔ Go beyond basic macros and look at some advanced techniques for navigating ranges through with VBA.

- ✔ See how macros can automate the selection and manipulation of specific cells.

- ✔ Explore how you can use macros to clean and transform the data in your workbooks.

- ✔ Uncover techniques that can help you automate the data exports.

Chapter 6

Feeling at Home on the Range

In This Chapter

▶ Selecting ranges

▶ Navigating the cells in your worksheets

▶ Inserting and deleting blank rows and columns

▶ Limiting range movement

▶ Finding and selecting the first blank row or column

*O*ne of the most important things you do in Excel is navigate the worksheet. When you work with Excel manually, you're constantly navigating to appropriate ranges, finding the last row, moving to the last column, hiding and unhiding ranges, and so on.

When you attempt to automate your work through VBA, you'll find that navigating your spreadsheet remains an important part of the automation process. In many cases, you need to dynamically navigate and manipulate Excel ranges, just as you would manually — only through VBA code. This chapter provides some of the most commonly used macros in terms of navigating and working with ranges.

Selecting and Formatting a Range

One of the basic things you need to do in VBA is to select a specific range to do something with it. The simple macro in this section selects the range D5:D16.

How the macro works

In this macro, you explicitly define the range to select by using the Range object:

```
Sub Macro1()

Range("D5:D16").Select

End Sub
```

After the range of cells is selected, you can use any of the Range properties to manipulate the cells. The macro has been altered so that the range is colored yellow, converted to number formatting, and bold.

```
Sub Macro1()

    Range("D5:D16").Select
    Selection.NumberFormat = "#,##0"
    Selection.Font.Bold = True
    Selection.Interior.ColorIndex = 36

End Sub
```

You don't have to memorize all the properties of the cell object to manipulate them. You can simply record a macro, do your formatting, and then look at the code that Excel has written. After you've seen what the correct syntax is, you can apply it as needed. Many Excel programmers start learning VBA this way.

Note that I refer to Selection several times in the preceding sample code. To write more efficient code, you can simply refer to the range, using the With-End With statement. This statement tells Excel that any action you perform applies to the object to which you've pointed. Note that this macro doesn't select the range. This point is key. In a macro, you can work with a range without selecting it first.

```
Sub Macro1()

    With Range("D5:D16")
        .NumberFormat = "#,##0"
        .Font.Bold = True
        .Interior.ColorIndex = 36
    End With

End Sub
```

Another way you can select a range is by using the Cells item of the Range object. The Cells item gives you a handy way to select ranges through code. It requires only relative row and column positions as parameters. Cells(5,4) translates to row 5, column 4 (or Cell D5). Cells(16, 4) translates to row 16, column 4 (or cell D16).

If you want to select a range of cells, simply pass two items to the Range object. This macro performs the same selection of range D5:D16:

```
Sub Macro1()

Range(Cells(5, 4), Cells(16, 4)).Select

End Sub
```

Here is the full formatting code using the Cells item. Again, note that this macro doesn't select the range you are altering. You can work with a range without selecting it first.

```
Sub Macro1()

    With Range(Cells(5, 4), Cells(16, 4))
        .NumberFormat = "#,##0"
        .Font.Bold = True
        .Interior.ColorIndex = 36
    End With

End Sub
```

How to use the macro

To implement this kind of a macro, you can copy and paste it into a standard module:

1. **Activate Visual Basic Editor by pressing Alt+F11.**
2. **Right-click the project/workbook name in the project window.**
3. **Choose Insert⇨Module.**
4. **Type or paste the code into the code window.**

Creating and Selecting Named Ranges

One of the more useful features in Excel is the capability to name your range (that is, to give your range a user-friendly name, so that you can more easily identify and refer to it via VBA).

Here are the steps you would perform to create a named range manually.

1. **Select the range you want to name.**

2. **Go to the Formulas tab in the Ribbon, and choose the Define Name command (see Figure 6-1).**

3. **In the New Name dialog box, give the chosen range a user-friendly name, as shown in Figure 6-2.**

4. **Click OK.**

   Your range is named.

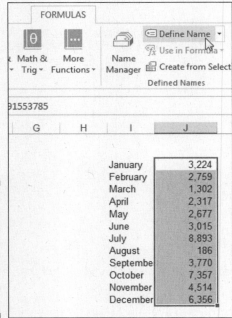

Figure 6-1:
Click the
Define
Name
command
to name
a chosen
range.

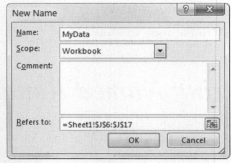

Figure 6-2:
Give your
range a
name.

To confirm that your named range was created properly, you can go to the Formula tab and select the Name Manager command. The Name Manager dialog box appears, as shown in Figure 6-3, and you can see all applied named ranges.

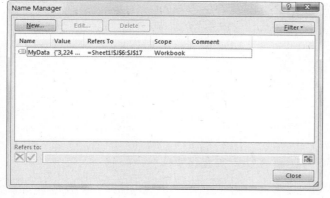

Figure 6-3:
The Name Manager dialog box lists all applied named ranges.

Creating a named range through VBA is much less involved. You can directly define the Name property of the Range object:

```
Sub Macro1()

Range("I1:J17").Name = "MyData"

End Sub
```

Admittedly, you'd be hard-pressed to find a situation where you would need to automate the creation of named ranges. The real efficiency comes in manipulating them through VBA.

How the macro works

In this macro, you simply pass the name of the range through the Range object. This object allows you to select the range:

```
Sub Macro1()

Range("MyData").Select

End Sub
```

As with normal ranges, you can refer to the range using the With-End With statement, which tells Excel that any action you perform applies to the object to which you've pointed. This technique not only prevents you from having to repeat syntax but also allows for the easy addition of actions by simply adding them between the With and End With statements.

```
Sub Macro1()

    With Range("MyData")
        .NumberFormat = "#,##0"
        .Font.Bold = True
        .Interior.ColorIndex = 36
    End With

End Sub
```

How to use the macro

To implement this kind of a macro, you can copy and paste it into a standard module:

1. **Activate Visual Basic Editor by pressing Alt+F11.**
2. **Right-click the project/workbook name in the project window.**
3. **Choose Insert⇨Module.**
4. **Type or paste the code.**

Enumerating through a Range of Cells

One must-have VBA skill is the capability to enumerate (or loop) through a range. If you do any serious macro work in Excel, you'll soon encounter the need to go through a range of cells one by one and perform some action.

The basic macro in this section shows you a simple way to enumerate through a range.

How the macro works

This macro uses two Range object variables. One variable captures the scope of data you're working with, and the other holds each individual cell as you go through the range. Then you use the For Each statement to activate, or bring into focus, each cell in the target range:

```
Sub Macro1()

'Step 1:  Declare your variables
    Dim MyRange As Range
    Dim MyCell As Range

'Step 2:  Define the target range
    Set MyRange = Range("D6:D17")

'Step 3:  Start looping through the range
    For Each MyCell In MyRange

'Step 4:  Do something with each cell

    If MyCell.Value > 3000 Then
        MyCell.Font.Bold = True
    End If

'Step 5: Get the next cell in the range
    Next MyCell

End Sub
```

The macro first declares two Range object variables. MyRange holds the entire target range, and MyCell holds each cell in the range as the macro enumerates through them one by one.

In Step 2, you fill the MyRange variable with the target range. In this example, you use Range("D6:D17"). If your target range is a named range, you could simply enter its name — Range("MyNamedRange").

In Step 3, the macro starts looping through each cell in the target range, activating each cell as it goes through.

After a cell is activated, you would do something with it. That "something" depends on the task at hand. You may want to delete rows when the active cell has a certain value, or you may want to insert a row between each active cell. In Step 4 of this example, the macro is changing the font to Bold for any cell that has a value greater than 3,000.

In Step 5, the macro loops back to get the next cell. After all cells in the target range are activated, the macro ends.

How to use the macro

To implement this macro, you can copy and paste it into a standard module:

1. **Activate Visual Basic Editor by pressing Alt+F11.**
2. **Right-click the project/workbook name in the project window.**
3. **Choose Insert⇨Module.**
4. **Type or paste the code.**

Inserting Blank Rows in a Range

Occasionally, you may need to dynamically insert rows into your data set. Although blank rows are generally bothersome, in some situations the final formatted version of your report requires blank rows to separate data. The macro in this section adds blank rows into a range.

How the macro works

This macro performs a reverse loop through the chosen range by using a counter. It starts at the last row of the range, inserting two blank rows, and then moves to the previous row in the range. It keeps doing the same insert for every loop, each time incrementing the counter to the previous row.

```vba
Sub Macro1()

'Step 1:  Declare your variables
    Dim MyRange As Range
    Dim iCounter As Long

'Step 2:  Define the target range
    Set MyRange = Range("C6:D17")

'Step 3:  Start reverse looping through the range
    For iCounter = MyRange.Rows.Count To 2 Step -1

'Step 4: Insert two blank rows
    MyRange.Rows(iCounter).EntireRow.Insert
    MyRange.Rows(iCounter).EntireRow.Insert

'Step 5: Go to the next counter number
    Next iCounter

End Sub
```

First, you declare two variables. The first variable is an Object variable called MyRange that defines the target range. The other variable is a Long Integer variable called iCounter that serves as an incremental counter.

In Step 2, the macro fills the MyRange variable with the target range. In this example, you use Range("C6:D17"). If your target range is a named range, you could simply enter its name — Range("MyNamedRange"). The macro sets the parameters for the incremental counter to start at the max count for the range (MyRange.Rows.Count) and end at 2 (the second row of the chosen range). Note that you are using the Step-1 qualifier, so Excel knows that you will adjust the counter backwards, moving back one increment on each iteration. In all, Step 3 tells Excel to start at the last row of the chosen range, moving backward until it gets to the second row of the range.

When working with a range, you can explicitly call out a specific row in the range by passing a row index number to the Rows collection of the range. For instance, Range("D6:D17").Rows(5) points to the fifth row in the range D6:D17.

In Step 4, the macro uses the iCounter variable as an index number for the Rows collection of MyRange. This variable helps pinpoint the exact row that the macro is working with in the current loop. The macro then uses the EntireRow.Insert method to insert a new blank row. Because you want two blank rows, you apply the EntireRow.Insert method twice.

In Step 5, the macro loops back to move to the next counter number.

How to use the macro

To implement this macro, you can copy and paste it into a standard module:

1. **Activate Visual Basic Editor by pressing Alt+F11.**
2. **Right-click the project/workbook name in the project window.**
3. **Choose Insert➪Module.**
4. **Type or paste the code.**

Unhiding All Rows and Columns

When you're auditing a spreadsheet that you did not create, you often want to ensure that you're getting a full view of the spreadsheet's contents. To do so, all columns and rows must not be hidden. This simple macro automatically unhides all rows and columns for you.

How the macro works

In this macro, you call on the Columns collection and the Rows collection of the worksheet. Each collection has properties that dictate where their objects are hidden or visible. Running this macro unhides every column in the Columns collection and every row in the Rows collection.

```
Sub Macro1()

Columns.EntireColumn.Hidden = False
Rows.EntireRow.Hidden = False

End Sub
```

How to use the macro

The best place to store this macro is in your personal macro workbook so that the macro is always available to you. The personal macro workbook is loaded whenever you start Excel. In VBE project window, it is named personal.xlsb.

1. **Activate Visual Basic Editor by pressing Alt+F11.**
2. **Right-click personal.xlb in the project window.**
3. **Choose Insert⇨Module.**
4. **Type or paste the code.**

If you don't see personal.xlb in your project window, the file doesn't exist yet. You'll have to record a macro, using personal macro workbook as the destination.

To record the macro in your personal macro workbook, display the Record Macro dialog box before you start recording. Then click the Store Macro In drop-down box and select the Personal Macro Workbook option. Then simply record a few cell clicks and then stop recording. You can discard the recorded macro and replace it with this one.

Deleting Blank Rows

Work with Excel long enough, and you'll find that blank rows can often cause havoc on many levels. They can create problems with formulas, introduce risk when copying and pasting, and sometimes cause strange behaviors in pivot tables. If you find that you are manually searching out and deleting blank rows in your data sets, the macro in this section can help automate the task.

How the macro works

In this macro, you use the UsedRange property of the ActiveSheet object to define the range you are working with. The UsedRange property gives you a range that encompasses the cells that have been used to enter data. You then establish a counter that starts at the last row of the used range and checks to see if the entire row is empty. If the entire row is indeed empty, you remove the row. You keep doing the same delete for every loop, each time incrementing the counter to the previous row.

```vba
Sub Macro1()

'Step 1:  Declare your variables
    Dim MyRange As Range
    Dim iCounter As Long

'Step 2:  Define the target range
    Set MyRange = ActiveSheet.UsedRange

'Step 3:  Start reverse looping through the range
    For iCounter = MyRange.Rows.Count To 1 Step -1

'Step 4: If entire row is empty delete it
        If Application.CountA(Rows(iCounter).EntireRow) = 0
            Then
        Rows(iCounter).Delete
        End If

'Step 5: Move to the next counter number
    Next iCounter

End Sub
```

The macro first declares two variables. The first variable is an Object variable called MyRange, which defines the target range. The other variable is a Long Integer variable called iCounter, which serves as an incremental counter.

In Step 2, the macro fills the MyRange variable with the UsedRange property of the ActiveSheet object. The UsedRange property gives you a range that encompasses the cells that have been used to enter data. Note that if you wanted to specify an actual range or a named range, you could simply enter its name — Range("MyNamedRange").

In this step, the macro sets the parameters for the incremental counter to start at the max count for the range (MyRange.Rows.Count) and end at 1 (the first row of the chosen range). Note that you use the Step-1 qualifier, so Excel knows you are going to adjust the counter backwards, moving back one increment on each iteration. In all, Step 3 tells Excel to start at the last row of the chosen range and move backward until it gets to the first row of the range.

When working with a range, you can explicitly call out a specific row in the range by passing a row index number to the Rows collection of the range. For instance, Range("D6:D17").Rows(5) points to the fifth row in the range D6:D17.

In Step 4, the macro uses the iCounter variable as an index number for the Rows collection of MyRange. This variable helps pinpoint the row you are working with in the current loop. The macro checks to see whether the cells in that row are empty. If they are, the macro deletes the entire row.

In Step 5, the macro loops back to move to the next counter number.

How to use the macro

The best place to store this macro is in your personal macro workbook so that the macro is always available to you. The personal macro workbook is loaded whenever you start Excel. In VBE project window, it is named personal.xlsb.

1. **Activate Visual Basic Editor by pressing Alt+F11.**

2. **Right-click personal.xlb in the project window.**

3. **Choose Insert⇨Module.**

4. **Type or paste the code.**

If you don't see personal.xlb in your project window, the file doesn't exist yet. You'll have to record a macro, using personal macro workbook as the destination.

To record the macro in your personal macro workbook, display the Record Macro dialog box before you start recording. Then click the Store Macro In drop-down box and select the Personal Macro Workbook option. Next, record a few cell clicks and then stop recording. You can discard the recorded macro and replace it with this one.

Deleting Blank Columns

Just as with blank rows, blank columns have the potential of causing unforeseen errors. If you find that you are manually searching for and deleting blank columns in your data sets, use the macro in this section to automate that task.

How the macro works

In this macro, you use the UsedRange property of the ActiveSheet object to define the range you are working with. The UsedRange property gives you a range that encompasses the cells that have been used to enter data. You then establish a counter that starts at the last column of the used range, checking to see if the entire column is empty. If the entire column is indeed empty, you remove the column. You keep doing the same delete for every loop, each time incrementing the counter to the previous column.

```
Sub Macro1()

'Step 1:  Declare your variables
    Dim MyRange As Range
    Dim iCounter As Long

'Step 2:  Define the target range
    Set MyRange = ActiveSheet.UsedRange

'Step 3:  Start reverse looping through the range
    For iCounter = MyRange.Columns.Count To 1 Step -1

'Step 4: If entire column is empty delete it
    If
        Application.CountA(Columns(iCounter).
        EntireColumn) = 0 Then
    Columns(iCounter).Delete
    End If

'Step 5: Move to the next counter number
    Next iCounter

End Sub
```

You first declare two variables. The first variable is an Object variable called MyRange, which defines the target range. The other variable is a Long Integer variable called iCounter, which serves as your incremental counter.

In Step 2, you fill the MyRange variable with the UsedRange property of the ActiveSheet object. The UsedRange property gives you a range that encompasses the cells that have been used to enter data. Note that if you wanted to specify an actual range or a named range, you could simply enter its name — Range("MyNamedRange").

In this step, you set the parameters for your incremental counter to start at the max count for the range (MyRange.Columns.Count) and end at 1 (the first row of the chosen range). Note that you are using the Step-1 qualifier, so Excel knows that you will increment the counter backwards, moving back one increment on each iteration. In all, Step 3 tells Excel that you want to start at the last column of the chosen range and move backward until you get to the first column of the range.

When working with a range, you can explicitly call out a specific column in the range by passing a column index number to the Columns collection of the range. For instance, Range("A1:D17").Columns(2) points to the second column in the range (column B).

In Step 4, the macro uses the iCounter variable as an index number for the Columns collection of MyRange. This variable helps pinpoint the column you are working with in the current loop. The macro checks to see whether all the cells in that column are empty. If they are, the macro deletes the entire column.

In Step 5, the macro loops back to increment the counter down.

How to use the macro

The best place to store this macro is in your personal macro workbook so that the macro is always available to you. The personal macro workbook is loaded whenever you start Excel. In VBE project window, it is named personal.xlsb.

1. **Activate Visual Basic Editor by pressing Alt+F11.**

2. **Right-click personal.xlb in the project window.**

3. **Choose Insert⇨Module.**

4. **Type or paste the code.**

If you don't see personal.xlb in your project window, the file doesn't exist yet. You'll have to record a macro, using personal macro workbook as the destination.

To record the macro in your personal macro workbook, display the Record Macro dialog box before you start recording. Then click the Store Macro In drop-down box and select Personal Macro Workbook. Simply record a few cell clicks and then stop recording. You can discard the recorded macro and replace it with this one.

Limiting Range Movement to a Particular Area

Excel gives you the ability to limit the range of cells that a user can scroll through. The macro demonstrated in this section is one you can easily implement today.

How the macro works

Excel's ScrollArea property allows you to set the scroll area for a particular worksheet. For instance, the following statement sets the scroll area on Sheet1 so the user cannot activate any cells outside A1:M17:

```
Sheets("Sheet1").ScrollArea = "A1:M17"
```

Because this setting is not saved with a workbook, you'll have to reset it each time the workbook is opened. You can accomplish this task by implementing the following statement in the Workbook_Open event:

```
Private Sub Worksheet_Open()

Sheets("Sheet1").ScrollArea = "A1:M17"

End Sub
```

If for some reason you need to clear the scroll area limits, you can remove the restriction with this statement:

```
ActiveSheet.ScrollArea = ""
```

How to use the macro

To implement this macro, you will need to copy and paste it into the Workbook_Open event code window. By placing the macro here, you allow it to run each time the workbook opens.

1. **Activate Visual Basic Editor by pressing Alt+F11.**

2. **In the project window, find your project/workbook name and click the plus sign next to it to see all the sheets.**

3. **Click ThisWorkbook.**

4. **In the Event drop-down box, select the Open event (see Figure 6-4).**

5. **Type or paste the code.**

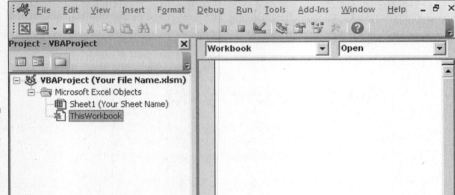

Figure 6-4:
Enter your
code in the
Workbook
Open event.

Selecting and Formatting All Formulas in a Workbook

When auditing an Excel workbook, it's paramount to have a firm grasp of all the formulas in each sheet. This means finding all the formulas, which can be an arduous task if performed manually.

However, Excel provides a slick way of finding and tagging all formulas in a worksheet. The macro in this section exploits this functionality to dynamically find all cells that contain formulas.

How the macro works

Excel has a set of predefined special cells that you can select by using the Go to Special dialog box. To select special cells manually, go to the Home tab on the Ribbon and select Go to Special. The Go to Special dialog box appears, as shown in Figure 6-5.

Figure 6-5:
The Go to
Special
dialog box.

In this dialog box, you can select a set of cells based on a few defining attributes, including formulas. Selecting the Formulas option effectively selects all cells that contain formulas (see Figure 6-6). At this point, you can color the cells to indicate they contain a formula.

The macro programmatically does the same thing for the entire workbook at the same time. Here, you use the SpecialCells method of the Cells collection. The SpecialCells method requires a type parameter that represents the type of special cell. In this case, you're using xlCellTypeFormulas.

In short, you refer to a special range that consists only of cells that contain a formula. You refer to this special range using the With-End With statement, which tells Excel that any action you perform applies only to the range to which you've pointed. Here, you're coloring the interior of the cells in the chosen range.

Figure 6-6:
Choose
Formulas
to tell Excel
to select
all cells
containing a
formula.

	A	B	C	D	E	F	G
5							
6	$719.20	6	$ 119.87				
7							
8					$867.59	6	$ 144.60
9							
10							
11							
12	$479.46	4	$ 79.91		$578.40	4	$ 96.40
13							
14							
15					$2,210.24	12	$ 368.37
16	$722.99	5	$ 120.50				

```
Sub Macro1()

'Step 1:  Declare your variables
    Dim ws As Worksheet

'Step 2: Avoid error if no formulas are found
    On Error Resume Next

'Step 3:  Start looping through worksheets
    For Each ws In ActiveWorkbook.Worksheets

'Step 4:  Select cells and highlight them
    With ws.Cells.SpecialCells(xlCellTypeFormulas)
    .Interior.ColorIndex = 36
    End With

'Step 5: Get next worksheet
    Next ws

End Sub
```

Step 1 declares an object called ws. This step creates a memory container for each worksheet the macro loops through.

If no formulas are in the spreadsheet, Excel will throw an error. In Step 2 you tell Excel to continue with the macro if an error is triggered.

Step 3 begins the looping, telling Excel to evaluate all worksheets in the active workbook.

In Step 4, the macro selects all cells containing formulas and then formats them.

In Step 5, you loop back to get the next sheet. After all sheets are evaluated, the macro ends.

How to use the macro

The best place to store this macro is in your personal macro workbook so that the macro is always available. The personal macro workbook is loaded whenever you start Excel. In VBE project window, it's named personal.xlsb.

1. **Activate Visual Basic Editor by pressing Alt+F11.**

2. **Right-click personal.xlb in the project window.**

3. **Choose Insert⇨Module.**

4. **Type or paste the code.**

If you don't see personal.xlb in your project window, the file doesn't exist yet. You'll have to record a macro, using personal macro workbook as the destination.

To record the macro in your personal macro workbook, display the Record Macro dialog box before you start recording. Then click the Store Macro In drop-down box and select Personal Macro Workbook. Then record a few cell clicks and then stop recording. You can discard the recorded macro and replace it with this one.

Finding and Selecting the First Blank Row or Column

You may often run across scenarios where you have to append rows or columns to an existing data set. When you want to append rows, you'll need to be able to find the last used row and then move down to the next empty cell (as shown in Figure 6-7). Likewise, when you want to append columns, you need to be able to find the last used column and then move over to the next empty cell.

Figure 6-7:
Use a macro to dynamically find the first available cell in a row or a column.

	A	B	C	D	E	F	G
5		January	February	March	April	May	June
6	Product 1	72,542	70,916	49,289	3,538	87,442	61,69
7	Product 2	28,187	18,175	71,645	99,211	10,516	91,07
8	Product 3	75,043	8,280	24,234	40,255	77,472	85,50
9	Product 4	4,984	31,805	47,905	45,292	89,648	94,80
10	Product 5	42,680	47,574	35,982	18,860	56,353	91,80
11	Product 6	16,140	3,676	76,712	27,619	68,199	36,28
12	Product 7	97,001	56,895	40,052	79,893	78,703	40,25
13	Product 8	21,227	28,168	97,923	16,585	1,843	98,59
14	Product 9	56,692	17,489	82,649	28,960	68,233	21,50
15	Product 10	64,906	54,698	93,271	29,388	29,712	54,32
16	Product 11	68,672	29,475	58,379	16,282	2,953	69,43
17	Product 12	38,676	1,457	3,833	98,225	99,695	2,71
18							

The macros in this section allow you to dynamically find and select the first blank row or column.

How the macro works

These macros both use the Cells item and the Offset property as key navigation tools.

The Cells item belongs to the Range object and provides a handy way to select ranges through code. It requires only relative row and column positions as parameters. Cells(5,4) translates to row 5, column 4 (or Cell D5). Cells(16, 4) translates to row 16, column 4 (or cell D16).

In addition to passing hard numbers to the Cells item, you can also pass expressions.

Cells(Rows.Count, 1) is the same as selecting the last row in the spreadsheet and the first column in the spreadsheet. In Excel, that essentially translates to cell A1048576.

Cells(1, Columns.Count) is the same as selecting the first row in the spreadsheet and the last column in the spreadsheet. In Excel, that translates to cell XFD1.

Combining the Cells statement with the End property enables Excel to jump to the last used row or column. This statement is equivalent to going to cell A1048576 and pressing Ctrl+Shift+up arrow on the keyboard. When you run this line of code, Excel automatically jumps to the last used row in column A:

```
Cells(Rows.Count, 1).End(xlUp).Select
```

Running this statement is equivalent to going to cell XFD1 and pressing Ctrl+Shift+left arrow on the keyboard. This line of code gets you to the last used column in row 1:

```
Cells(1, Columns.Count).End(xlToLeft).Select
```

When you get to the last used row or column, you can use the Offset property to move down or over to the next blank row or column. The Offset property uses a row and column index to specify a changing base point.

For example, the following statement selects cell A2 because the row index in the offset is moving the row base point by 1:

```
Range("A1").Offset(1, 0).Select
```

This statement selects cell C4 because the row and column indexes move the base point by three rows and two columns:

```
Range("A1").Offset(3, 2).Select
```

Pulling all these concepts together, you can create a macro that selects the first blank row or column.

This macro selects the first blank row:

```
Sub Macro1()

'Step 1:  Declare your variables
    Dim LastRow As Long

'Step 2:  Capture the last-used row number
    LastRow = Cells(Rows.Count, 1).End(xlUp).Row

'Step 3:  Select the next row down
    Cells(LastRow, 1).Offset(1, 0).Select
End Sub
```

First, you declare a Long Integer variable called LastRow to hold the row number of the last used row.

In Step 2, you capture the last used row by starting at the last row in the worksheet and using the End property to jump up to the first nonempty cell (the equivalent of going to cell A1048576 and pressing Ctrl+Shift+up arrow).

In Step 3, you use the Offset property to move down one row and select the first blank cell in column A.

This macro selects the first blank column:

```
Sub Macro1()

'Step 1:  Declare your variables
    Dim LastColumn As Long

'Step 2:  Capture the last-used column number
    LastColumn = Cells(5,
            Columns.Count).End(xlToLeft).Column

'Step 3:  Select the next column over
    Cells(5, LastColumn).Offset(0, 1).Select

End Sub
```

First, you declare a Long Integer variable called LastColumn to hold the column number of the last used column.

In Step 2, you capture the last used column by starting at the last column in the worksheet and using the End property to jump up to the first nonempty column (the equivalent of going to cell XFD5 and pressing Ctrl+Shift+left arrow).

In Step 3, you use the Offset property to move over one column and select the first blank column in row 5.

How to use the macro

You can implement these macros by pasting them into a standard module:

1. **Activate Visual Basic Editor by pressing Alt+F11.**
2. **Right-click the project/workbook name in the project window.**
3. **Choose Insert⇨Module.**
4. **Type or paste the code.**

Chapter 7

Manipulating Data with Macros

. . . .

In This Chapter

▶ Converting values in a range

▶ Trimming and truncating text

▶ Replacing blanks cells with values

▶ Adding text to existing values

▶ Handling duplicates in a range

▶ Working with AutoFilter drop-downs

. . . .

*W*hen working with information in Excel, you often have to transform the data, cleaning, standardizing, or shaping it in ways that are appropriate for your work. Transforming data can mean anything from cleaning out extra spaces to padding numbers with zeros to filtering data for certain criteria.

This chapter shows you some of the more useful macros you can use to dynamically transform the data in your workbooks. If you like, you can combine these macros into one, running each piece of code in a sequence that essentially automates the scrubbing and shaping of your data.

Copying and Pasting a Range

One of the basic data manipulation skills you'll need to learn is copying and pasting a range of data. Doing this manually is fairly easy. Luckily, it's just as easy to copy and paste by using VBA.

How the macro works

In this macro, you use the Copy method of the Range object to copy data from D6:D17 and paste to L6:L17. Note the use of the Destination argument, which tells Excel where to paste the data:

```
Sub Macro1()

Sheets("Sheet1").Range("D6:D17").Copy _
Destination:=Sheets("Sheet1").Range("L6:L17")

End Sub
```

When working with your spreadsheet, you likely often have to copy formulas and paste them as values. To do this in a macro, you can use the PasteSpecial method. In this example, you copy the formulas F6:F17 to M6:M17. Note that you're not only pasting as values by using xlPasteValues but also applying the formatting from the copied range by using xlPasteFormats.

```
Sub Macro1()

Sheets("Sheet1").Range("F6:F17").Copy
Sheets("Sheet1").Range("M6:M17").PasteSpecial
        xlPasteValues
Sheets("Sheet1").Range("M6:M17").PasteSpecial
        xlPasteFormats

End Sub
```

Keep in mind that the ranges and sheet names specified here are for demonstration. Alter them to suit the data in your worksheet.

How to use the macro

To implement this macro, you can copy and paste it into a standard module:

1. **Activate Visual Basic Editor by pressing Alt+F11.**

2. **Right-click the project/workbook name in the project window.**

3. **Choose Insert ⇨ Module.**

4. **Type or paste the code.**

Converting All Formulas in a Range to Values

Sometimes, you may want to apply formulas in a certain workbook, but you don't necessarily want to keep or distribute the formulas with your workbook. In these situations, you may want to convert all the formulas in a given range to values.

How the macro works

In this macro, you essentially use two Range object variables. One of the variables captures the scope of data you are working with, whereas the other is used to hold each individual cell as you go through the range. Then you use the For Each statement to activate or bring each cell in the target range into focus. Every time a cell is activated, you check to see whether the cell contains a formula. If it does, you replace the formula with the value shown in the cell.

```
Sub Macro1()

'Step 1: Declare your variables
  Dim MyRange As Range
  Dim MyCell As Range


'Step 2: Save the workbook
 before changing cells?
  Select Case MsgBox("Can't Undo this action. " & _
       "Save Workbook First?", vbYesNoCancel)
    Case Is = vbYes
    ThisWorkbook.Save

    Case Is = vbCancel
    Exit Sub
  End Select


'Step 3: Define the target range
  Set MyRange = Selection


'Step 4: Start looping through the range
  For Each MyCell In MyRange


'Step 5: If cell has formula, set to the value shown
  If MyCell.HasFormula Then
  MyCell.Formula = MyCell.Value
  End If
```

```
'Step 6: Get the next cell in the range
  Next MyCell

End Sub
```

Step 1 declares two Range object variables. MyRange holds the entire target range, and MyCell holds each cell in the range as you enumerate through them one by one.

When you run a macro, it destroys the undo stack, so you can't undo the changes a macro makes. Because you're changing data, you need the option of saving the workbook before running the macro. Step 2 performs this task. You call up a message box that asks if you want to save the workbook first. You have three choices: Yes, No, and Cancel. Clicking Yes saves the workbook and continues with the macro. Clicking Cancel exits the procedure without running the macro. Clicking No runs the macro without saving the workbook.

Step 3 fills the MyRange variable with the target range. In this example, you use the selected range — the range that was selected on the spreadsheet. You can easily set the MyRange variable to a specific range, such as Range("A1:Z100"). Also, if your target range is a named range, you could simply enter its name: Range("MyNamedRange").

Step 4 starts looping through each cell in the target range, activating each cell as it goes through.

After a cell is activated, the macro uses the HasFormula property in Step 5 to check whether the cell contains a formula. If it does, you set the cell to equal the value shown in the cell. This effectively replaces the formula with a hard-coded value.

Step 6 loops back to get the next cell. After all cells in the target range are activated, the macro ends.

How to use the macro

To implement this macro, you can copy and paste it into a standard module:

1. **Activate Visual Basic Editor by pressing Alt+F11.**

2. **Right-click the project/workbook name in the project window.**

3. **Choose Insert ⇨ Module.**

4. **Type or paste the code.**

Performing the Text to Columns Command on All Columns

When you import data from other sources, you may wind up with cells where the number values are formatted as text. You typically recognize this problem because no matter what you do, you can't format the numbers in these cells to numeric, currency, or percentage formats. You may also see a smart tag on the cells that tells you the cell is formatted as text, as shown in Figure 7-1.

Figure 7-1:
Sometimes imported numbers are formatted as text.

B	C	D	E	F	G	H
	June	3015.29997101164	42	71.79		
	July	8892.72320795156	41	216.9		
	August	3185.53161972604	41	77.7		
	Septemb	The number in this cell is formatted as text or preceded by an apostrophe.				
	October	7357.41604042586	40	183.94		
	November	4514.43505181198	39	115.75		
	December	6355.67839756981	43	147.81		

It's easy enough to fix this manually by clicking the Text to Columns command on the Data tab (see Figure 7-2). The Text to Columns Wizard dialog box appears, as shown in Figure 7-3. You don't need to go through all the steps in this wizard; simply click the Finish button to apply the fix.

Figure 7-2:
Click the Text to Columns command.

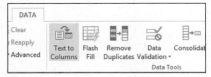

Although the Text to Columns fix is simple, Excel doesn't let you perform this action on multiple columns. You have to apply the fix one column at a time, which is a nuisance when you have this issue in many columns.

This section provides a simple macro that can help save your sanity.

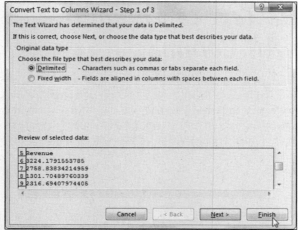

Figure 7-3:
Click
Finish to fix
incorrectly
formatted
numbers.

How the macro works

In this macro, you use two Range object variables to go through your target range, leveraging the For Each statement to activate each cell in the target range. Every time a cell is activated, you simply reset the value of the cell. This macro in effect does the same thing as the Text to Columns command.

```
Sub Macro1()

'Step 1: Declare your variables
  Dim MyRange As Range
  Dim MyCell As Range


'Step 2: Save the workbook before changing cells?
  Select Case MsgBox("Can't Undo this action. " & _
           "Save Workbook First?", vbYesNoCancel)
    Case Is = vbYes
    ThisWorkbook.Save

    Case Is = vbCancel
    Exit Sub
  End Select


'Step 3: Define the target range
  Set MyRange = Selection


'Step 4: Start looping through the range
  For Each MyCell In MyRange
```

```
'Step 5: Reset the cell value
   If Not IsEmpty(MyCell) Then
   MyCell.Value = MyCell.Value
   End If


'Step 6: Get the next cell in the range
   Next MyCell

End Sub
```

Step 1 declares two Range object variables. The MyRange variable holds the entire target range, and the MyCell variable holds each cell in the range as the macro enumerates through them one by one.

When you run a macro, it destroys the undo stack, so you can't undo the changes a macro makes. Because the macro is changing data, you need the option of saving the workbook before running the macro. Step 2 performs this task. Here, you display a message box that asks if you want to save the workbook first. You have three choices: Yes, No, and Cancel. Clicking Yes saves the workbook and continues with the macro. Clicking Cancel exits the procedure without running the macro. Clicking No runs the macro without saving the workbook.

Step 3 fills the MyRange variable with the target range. In this example, you use the selected range — the range selected on the spreadsheet. You can easily set the MyRange variable to a specific range, such as Range("A1:Z100"). Also, if your target range is a named range, you could simply enter its name: Range("MyNamedRange").

Step 4 starts looping through each cell in the target range, activating each cell as you go through.

After a cell is activated, the macro uses the IsEmpty function to make sure the cell is not empty. You do this to improve performance a little by skipping the cell if it's empty. You then simply reset the cell to its own value. This step removes any formatting mismatch.

Step 6 loops back to get the next cell. After all cells in the target range are activated, the macro ends.

How to use the macro

To implement this macro, you can copy and paste it into a standard module:

1. **Activate Visual Basic Editor by pressing Alt+F11.**
2. **Right-click the project/workbook name in the project window.**

3. **Choose Insert ➪ Module.**

4. **Type or paste the code.**

Converting Trailing Minus Signs

Legacy and mainframe systems are notorious for outputting trailing minus signs. In other words, instead of a number like –142, some systems output 142–. This obviously wreaks havoc on your spreadsheet — especially if you need to perform mathematic operations on the data. The nifty macro in this section goes through a target range and fixes all negative minus signs so that they show up in front of the number instead of at the end.

How the macro works

In this macro, you use two Range object variables to go through your target range, leveraging the For Each statement to activate each cell in the target range. Every time a cell is activated, you convert the value of the cell into a Double numeric data type by using the CDbl function. The Double data type forces any negative signs to appear at the front of the number.

```vba
Sub Macro1()

'Step 1: Declare your variables
  Dim MyRange As Range
  Dim MyCell As Range


'Step 2: Save the workbook before changing cells?
  Select Case MsgBox("Can't Undo this action. " & _
          "Save Workbook First?", vbYesNoCancel)
    Case Is = vbYes
    ThisWorkbook.Save

    Case Is = vbCancel
    Exit Sub
  End Select


'Step 3: Define the target range
  Set MyRange = Selection


'Step 4: Start looping through the range
  For Each MyCell In MyRange
```

```
'Step 5: Convert the value to a Double
  If IsNumeric(MyCell) Then
    MyCell = CDbl(MyCell)
  End If


'Step 6: Get the next cell in the range
  Next MyCell

End Sub
```

Step 1 declares two Range object variables. The MyRange variable holds the entire target range, and the MyCell variable holds each cell in the range as you enumerate through them one by one.

When you run a macro, it destroys the undo stack, so you can't undo the changes a macro makes. Because you're changing data, you need the option of saving the workbook before running the macro. Step 2 performs this task by displaying a message box that asks if you want to save the workbook first. You have three choices: Yes, No, and Cancel. Clicking Yes saves the workbook and continues with the macro. Clicking Cancel exits the procedure without running the macro. Clicking No runs the macro without saving the workbook.

Step 3 fills the MyRange variable with the target range. In this example, you use the selected range — the range selected on the spreadsheet. You can easily set the MyRange variable to a specific range, such as Range("A1:Z100"). Also, if your target range is a named range, you could simply enter its name — Range("MyNamedRange").

Step 4 starts looping through each cell in the target range, activating each cell as it goes through.

After a cell is activated, Step 5 uses the IsNumeric function to check to see whether the value can be evaluated as a number. This step ensures that you don't affect textual fields. You then pass the cell's value through the CDbl function, which converts the value to the Double numeric data type, forcing the minus sign to the front.

Step 6 loops back to get the next cell. After all cells in the target range are activated, the macro ends.

Because you define the target range as the current selection, you want to be sure to select the area where your data exists before running this code. You don't want to select the entire worksheet because every empty cell in the spreadsheet would be filled with a zero. To ensure that you don't have this problem, explicitly define the target range, such as Set MyRange = Range("A1:Z100").

How to use the macro

To implement this macro, you can copy and paste it into a standard module:

1. **Activate Visual Basic Editor by pressing Alt+F11.**
2. **Right-click the project/workbook name in the project window.**
3. **Choose Insert ⇨ Module.**
4. **Type or paste the code.**

Trimming Spaces from All Cells in a Range

A frequent problem when you import dates from other sources is leading or trailing spaces. That is, the imported values have spaces at the beginning or end of the cell. These extra spaces make it difficult to do things like VLOOKUP or sorting. Here is a macro that makes it easy to search for and remove extra spaces in your cells.

How the macro works

In this macro, you enumerate through a target range, passing each cell in that range through the Trim function:

```
Sub Macro1()

'Step 1: Declare your variables
  Dim MyRange As Range
  Dim MyCell As Range


'Step 2: Save the workbook before changing cells?
  Select Case MsgBox("Can't Undo this action. " & _
          "Save Workbook First?", vbYesNoCancel)

    Case Is = vbYes
    ThisWorkbook.Save

    Case Is = vbCancel
    Exit Sub
  End Select
```

```
'Step 3: Define the target range
   Set MyRange = Selection


'Step 4: Start looping through the range
   For Each MyCell In MyRange


'Step 5: Trim spaces
   If Not IsEmpty(MyCell) Then
   MyCell = Trim(MyCell)
   End If


'Step 6: Get the next cell in the range
   Next MyCell

End Sub
```

Step 1 declares two Range object variables. The MyRange variable holds the entire target range, and the MyCell variable holds each cell in the range as the macro enumerates through them one by one.

When you run a macro, it destroys the undo stack, so you can't undo the changes a macro makes. Because you're changing data, you need the option of saving the workbook before running the macro. Step 2 performs this task by displaying a message box that asks if you want to save the workbook first. Your three choices are Yes, No, and Cancel. Clicking Yes saves the workbook and continues with the macro. Clicking Cancel exits the procedure without running the macro. Clicking No runs the macro without saving the workbook.

Step 3 fills the MyRange variable with the target range. In this example, you use the selected range — the range selected on the spreadsheet. You can easily set the MyRange variable to a specific range, such as Range("A1:Z100"). Also, if your target range is a named range, you could simply enter its name — Range("MyNamedRange").

Step 4 starts looping through each cell in the target range, activating each cell as you go through.

After a cell is activated, the macro uses the IsEmpty function to make sure that the cell is not empty. This function improves performance a bit by skipping the cell if it's empty. You then pass the value of that cell to the Trim function, which is a native Excel function that removes leading and trailing spaces.

Step 6 loops back to get the next cell. After all cells in the target range are activated, the macro ends.

How to use the macro

To implement this macro, you can copy and paste it into a standard module:

1. **Activate Visual Basic Editor by pressing Alt+F11.**
2. **Right-click the project/workbook name in the project window.**
3. **Choose Insert ⇨ Module.**
4. **Type or paste the code.**

Truncating Zip Codes to the Left Five Digits

U.S. zip codes come in either 5 or 10 digits. Some systems output a 10-digit zip code, which is too many for a lot of Excel analysis. A common data standardization task is to truncate zip codes to the left five digits. Many of us use formulas to do this, but if you're constantly cleaning up your zip codes, you might want to use the macro outlined in this section to automate the task.

It's important to note that although this macro solves a specific problem, the concept of truncating data remains useful for many other types of data cleanup activities.

How the macro works

This macro uses the Left function to extract the left five characters of each zip code in the given range:

```
Sub Macro1()

'Step 1: Declare your variables
    Dim MyRange As Range
    Dim MyCell As Range


'Step 2: Save the workbook before changing cells?
    Select Case MsgBox("Can't Undo this action. " & _
            "Save Workbook First?", vbYesNoCancel)
        Case Is = vbYes
        ThisWorkbook.Save
```

```
      Case Is = vbCancel
      Exit Sub
   End Select


'Step 3: Define the target range
   Set MyRange = Selection


'Step 4: Start looping through the range
   For Each MyCell In MyRange


'Step 5: Extract the left 5 characters
   If Not IsEmpty(MyCell) Then
   MyCell = Left(MyCell, 5)
   End If


'Step 6: Get the next cell in the range
   Next MyCell

End Sub
```

Step 1 declares two Range object variables. MyRange holds the entire target range, and MyCell holds each cell in the range as the macro enumerates through them one by one.

When you run a macro, it destroys the undo stack, so you can't undo the changes a macro makes. Because you're changing data, you need the option of saving the workbook before running the macro. Step 2 performs this task by displaying a message box that asks if you want to save the workbook first. Your three choices are Yes, No, and Cancel. Clicking Yes saves the workbook and continues with the macro. Clicking Cancel exits the procedure without running the macro. Clicking No runs the macro without saving the workbook.

Step 3 fills the MyRange variable with the target range. In this example, you use the selected range — the range selected on the spreadsheet. You can easily set the MyRange variable to a specific range, such as Range("A1:Z100"). Also, if your target range is a named range, you could simply enter its name: Range("MyNamedRange").

Step 4 starts looping through each cell in the target range, activating each cell.

After a cell is activated, Step 5 uses the IsEmpty function to make sure that the cell is not empty. This function improves performance a bit by skipping the cell if it's empty. You then pass the cell's value through Left function, which allows you to extract out the nth leftmost characters in a string. In this scenario, you need the left five characters to truncate the zip code to five digits.

Step 6 loops back to get the next cell. After all the cells in the target range are activated, the macro ends.

As you may have guessed, you can also use the Right function to extract out the nth right-most characters in a string. As an example, it's not uncommon to work with product numbers where the first few characters hold a particular attribute or meaning, whereas the last few characters point to the actual product (as in 100-4567). You can extract out the actual product by using Right(Product_Number, 4).

Because you define the target range as the current selection, be sure to select the area where your data exists before running this code. In other words, you wouldn't want to select cells that don't conform to the logic you placed in this macro. Otherwise, every cell you select is truncated, whether you mean it to be or not. Of course, you can ensure this is never a problem by explicitly defining the target range, such as Set MyRange = Range("A1:Z100").

How to use the macro

To implement this macro, you can copy and paste it into a standard module:

1. **Activate Visual Basic Editor by pressing Alt+F11 on your keyboard.**

2. **Right-click project/workbook name in the project window.**

3. **Choose Insert ⇨ Module.**

4. **Type or paste the code.**

Padding Cells with Zeros

Many systems require unique identifiers (such as customer number, order number, or product number) to have a fixed character length. For instance, you frequently see customer numbers that look like this: 00000045478. This concept of taking a unique identifier and forcing it to have a fixed length is typically referred to as padding. The number is padded with zeros to achieve the prerequisite character length.

It's a pain to do this manually in Excel. However, with a macro, padding numbers with zeros is a breeze.

Some Excel gurus will be quick to point out that you can apply a custom number format to pad numbers with zeros by going to the Format Cells dialog box, selecting Custom on the Number tab, and entering "0000000000" as the custom format.

The problem with this solution is that the padding you get is cosmetic only. A quick glance at the formula bar will reveal that the data actually remains numeric without the padding (it does not become textual). So if you copy and paste the data into another platform or non-Excel table, you will lose the cosmetic padding.

How the macro works

Say that all your customer numbers need to be 10 characters long. So for each customer number, you need to pad the number with enough zeros to get it to 10 characters. This macro does just that.

As you review this macro, keep in mind that you need to change the padding logic in Step 5 to match your situation.

```
Sub Macro1()

'Step 1: Declare your variables
  Dim MyRange As Range
  Dim MyCell As Range


'Step 2: Save the workbook before changing cells?
  Select Case MsgBox("Can't Undo this action. " & _
          "Save Workbook First?", vbYesNoCancel)
    Case Is = vbYes
    ThisWorkbook.Save

    Case Is = vbCancel
    Exit Sub
  End Select


'Step 3: Define the target range
  Set MyRange = Selection


'Step 4: Start looping through the range
  For Each MyCell In MyRange


'Step 5: Pad with 10 zeros then take the right 10
  If Not IsEmpty(MyCell) Then
```

```
      MyCell.NumberFormat = "@"
      MyCell = "0000000000" & MyCell
      MyCell = Right(MyCell, 10)

   End If

 'Step 6: Get the next cell in the range
   Next MyCell

End Sub
```

Step 1 declares two Range object variables, one called MyRange to hold the entire target range, and the other called MyCell to hold each cell in the range as the macro enumerates through them one by one.

When you run a macro, it destroys the undo stack, meaning that you can't undo the changes a macro makes. Because you are actually changing data, you need to give yourself the option of saving the workbook before running the macro. This is what Step 2 does. Here, you call up a message box that asks if you want to save the workbook first. It then gives us three choices: Yes, No, and Cancel. Clicking Yes saves the workbook and continues with the macro. Clicking Cancel exits the procedure without running the macro. Clicking No runs the macro without saving the workbook.

Step 3 fills the MyRange variable with the target range. In this example, you use the selected range — the range that was selected on the spread-sheet. You can easily set the MyRange variable to a specific range such as Range("A1:Z100"). Also, if your target range is a named range, you could simply enter its name: Range("MyNamedRange").

Step 4 starts looping through each cell in the target range, activating each cell.

After a cell is activated, Step 5 uses the IsEmpty function to make sure the cell is not empty. You do this to save a little on performance by skipping the cell if there is nothing in it.

The macro then ensures that the cell is formatted as text. This because a cell formatted as a number cannot have leading zeros — Excel would automatically remove them. On the next line, you use the NumberFormat property to specify that the format is @. This symbol indicates text formatting.

Next, the macro concatenates the cell value with 10 zeros. You do this simply by explicitly entering 10 zeros in the code, and then using the ampersand (&) to combine them with the cell value.

Finally, Step 5 uses the Right function to extract out the 10 right-most characters. This effectively gives us the cell value, padded with enough zeros to make 10 characters.

Step 6 loops back to get the next cell. After all cells in the target range are activated, the macro ends.

How to use the macro

To implement this macro, you can copy and paste it into a standard module:

1. **Activate Visual Basic Editor by pressing Alt+F11 on your keyboard.**
2. **Right-click the project/workbook name in the project window.**
3. **Choose Insert ⇨ Module.**
4. **Type or paste the code.**

Replacing Blanks Cells with a Value

In some analyses, blank cells can cause of all kinds of trouble. They can cause sorting issues, they can prevent proper auto filling, they can cause your pivot tables to apply the Count function instead of the Sum function, and so on.

Blanks aren't always bad, but if they are causing you trouble, this is a macro you can use to quickly replace the blanks in a given range with a value that indicates a blank cell.

How the macro works

This macro enumerates through the cells in the given range, and then uses the Len function to check the length of the value in the active cell. Blank cells have a character length of 0. If the length is indeed 0, the macro enters a 0 in the cell, effectively replacing the blanks.

```
Sub Macro1()

'Step 1: Declare your variables
  Dim MyRange As Range
  Dim MyCell As Range

'Step 2: Save the workbook before changing cells?
  Select Case MsgBox("Can't Undo this action. " & _
          "Save Workbook First?", vbYesNoCancel)
    Case Is = vbYes
    ThisWorkbook.Save
```

```
      Case Is = vbCancel
        Exit Sub
    End Select


'Step 3: Define the target range
  Set MyRange = Selection


'Step 4: Start looping through the range
  For Each MyCell In MyRange


'Step 5: Ensure the cell has text formatting
  If Len(MyCell.Value) = 0 Then
  MyCell = 0
  End If


'Step 6: Get the next cell in the range
  Next MyCell

End Sub
```

You first declare two Range object variables, one called MyRange to hold the entire target range, and the other called MyCell to hold each cell in the range as the macro enumerates through them one by one.

When you run a macro, it destroys the undo stack. This means you can't undo the changes a macro makes. Because you are actually changing data, you need to give yourself the option of saving the workbook before running the macro. This is what Step 2 does. Here, you call up a message box that asks if you want to save the workbook first. It then gives us three choices: Yes, No, and Cancel. Clicking Yes saves the workbook and continues with the macro. Clicking Cancel exits the procedure without running the macro. Clicking No runs the macro without saving the workbook.

Step 3 fills the MyRange variable with the target range. In this example, you are using the selected range — the range that was selected on the spreadsheet. You can easily set the MyRange variable to a specific range such as Range("A1:Z100"). Also, if your target range is a named range, you could simply enter its name: Range("MyNamedRange").

Step 4 starts looping through each cell in the target range, activating each cell.

After a cell is activated, you use the IsEmpty function to make sure the cell is not empty. You do this to save a little on performance by skipping the cell if it's empty. You then use the Len function, which is a standard Excel function that returns a number corresponding to the length of the string being evaluated. If the cell is blank, the length with be 0, at which point, the macro replaces the blank with a 0. You could obviously replace the blank with any value you'd like (N/A, TBD, No Data, and so on).

Step 6 loops back to get the next cell. After all cells in the target range are activated, the macro ends.

Because you define the target range as the current selection, you want to be sure to select the area where your data exists before running this code. That is to say, you wouldn't want to select the entire worksheet. Otherwise, every empty cell in the spreadsheet would be filled with a zero. You can ensure that this is never a problem by explicitly defining a range, such as Set MyRange = Range("A1:Z100").

How to use the macro

To implement this macro, you can copy and paste it into a standard module:

1. **Activate Visual Basic Editor by pressing Alt+F11 on your keyboard.**
2. **Right-click the project/workbook name in the project window.**
3. **Choose Insert ⇨ Module.**
4. **Type or paste the code.**

Adding Text to the Left or Right of Your Cells

Every so often, you come upon a situation where you need to attach data to the beginning or end of the cells in a range. For instance, you may need to add an area code to a set of phone numbers. The macro in this section demonstrates how you can automate data standardization tasks that require adding data to values.

How the macro works

This macro uses two Range object variables to go through the target range, leveraging the For Each statement to activate each cell in the target range.

Every time a cell is activated, the macro attaches an area code to the beginning of the cell value.

```
Sub Macro1()

'Step 1: Declare your variables
  Dim MyRange As Range
  Dim MyCell As Range


'Step 2: Save the workbook before changing cells?
  Select Case MsgBox("Can't Undo this action. " & _
          "Save Workbook First?", vbYesNoCancel)
    Case Is = vbYes
    ThisWorkbook.Save

    Case Is = vbCancel
    Exit Sub
  End Select


'Step 3: Define the target range
  Set MyRange = Selection


'Step 4: Start looping through the range
  For Each MyCell In MyRange


'Step 5: Ensure the cell has text formatting
  If Not IsEmpty(MyCell) Then
  MyCell = "(972) " & MyCell
  End If


'Step 6: Get the next cell in the range
  Next MyCell

End Sub
```

Step 1 declares two Range object variables. MyRange holds the entire target range, and MyCell holds each cell in the range as you enumerate through them one by one.

When you run a macro, it destroys the undo stack, so you can't undo the changes a macro makes. Because you're changing data, you need the option of saving the workbook before running the macro. Step 2 displays a message box that asks if you want to save the workbook first. Your three choices are Yes, No, and Cancel. Clicking Yes saves the workbook and continues with the macro. Clicking Cancel exits the procedure without running the macro. Clicking No runs the macro without saving the workbook.

Step 3 fills the MyRange variable with the target range. In this example, you use the selected range — the range selected on the spreadsheet. You can easily set the MyRange variable to a specific range, such as Range("A1:Z100"). Also, if your target range is a named range, you could simply enter its name: Range("MyNamedRange").

Step 4 starts looping through each cell in the target range, activating each cell as you go through.

After a cell is activated, you use the ampersand (&) to combine an area code with the cell value. If you need to add text to the end of the cell value, you would simply place the ampersand and the text at the end. For instance, MyCell = MyCell & "Added Text".

Step 6 loops back to get the next cell. After all cells in the target range are activated, the macro ends.

How to use the macro

To implement this macro, you can copy and paste it into a standard module:

1. **Activate Visual Basic Editor by pressing Alt+F11.**
2. **Right-click the project/workbook name in the project window.**
3. **Choose Insert ⇨ Module.**
4. **Type or paste the code.**

Cleaning Up Nonprinting Characters

Sometimes your data has nonprinting characters, such as line feeds, carriage returns, and nonbreaking spaces. These characters often need to be removed before you can use the data for serious analysis.

Now, anyone who has worked with Excel for more than a month knows about the Find and Replace functionality. You may have even recorded a macro while performing a Find and Replace (a recorded macro is an excellent way to automate find-and-replace procedures). If so, your initial reaction may be to simply find and replace these characters. The problem is that nonprinting characters are for the most part invisible and thus difficult to clean up with normal Find and Replace routines. The easiest way to clean them up is through VBA.

If you find yourself struggling with those pesky invisible characters, use the general-purpose macro in this section to find and remove all nonprinting characters.

How the macro works

This macro is a relatively simple Find and Replace routine. You use the Replace method, telling Excel what to find and what to replace it with. The syntax is similar to what you would see when recording a macro while manually performing a Find and Replace. The difference is that instead of hard-coding the text to find, the macro uses character codes to specify your search text.

Every character has an underlying ASCII code, similar to a serial number. For instance, the lowercase letter *a* has an ASCII code of 97. The lowercase letter *c* has an ASCII code of 99. Likewise, invisible characters also have a code:

- ✔ The line-feed character code is 10.
- ✔ The carriage-return character code is 13.
- ✔ The nonbreaking-space character code is 160.

This macro utilizes the Replace method, passing each character's ASCII code as the search item. Each character code is then replaced with an empty string:

```
Sub Macro1()

'Step 1: Remove line feeds
  ActiveSheet.UsedRange.Replace What:=Chr(10), _
  Replacement:=""

'Step 2: Remove carriage returns
  ActiveSheet.UsedRange.Replace What:=Chr(13), _
  Replacement:=""

'Step 3: Remove nonbreaking spaces
  ActiveSheet.UsedRange.Replace What:=Chr(160), _
  Replacement:=""

End Sub
```

Step 1 looks for and removes the line-feed character, whose ASCII code is 10. You can identify the code 10 character by passing it through the Chr function. After Chr(10) is identified as the search item, this step passes an empty string to the Replacement argument.

Note the use of ActiveSheet.UsedRange, which essentially tells Excel to look in all the cells containing data. You can replace the UsedRange object with an actual range if needed.

Step 2 finds and removes the carriage-return character.

Step 3 finds and removes the nonbreaking-space character.

The characters covered in this macro are the most common nonprinting characters. If you work with others, simply add a new line of code, specifying the appropriate character code. You can enter "ASCII Code Listing" in any search engine to see a list the codes for various characters.

How to use the macro

To implement this macro, you can copy and paste it into a standard module:

1. **Activate Visual Basic Editor by pressing Alt+F11.**
2. **Right-click the project/workbook name in the project window.**
3. **Choose Insert ➪ Module.**
4. **Type or paste the code.**

Highlighting Duplicates in a Range of Data

Ever wanted to expose the duplicate values in a range? The macro in this section does just that. You can manually find and highlight duplicates in many ways: using formulas, conditional formatting, sorting, and so on. However, all these manual methods require setup and some level of maintenance as the data changes.

This macro simplifies the task, allowing you to find and highlight duplicates in your data with a click of the mouse, as shown in Figure 7-4.

Customers	Product Number
0000011112	C5567
0000046047	P8844
0000046047	R7609
0000047329	P8895
0000056510	P8867
0000058682	M2244
0000058682	C3322
0000058682	R7786
0000086362	M7765
0000086362	C8874
0000089129	M3345
0000090210	C5521

Figure 7-4:
Dynamically find and highlight duplicate values in a selected range.

How the macro works

The macro enumerates through the cells in the target range, leveraging the For Each statement to activate each cell one at a time. You then use the CountIf function to count the number of times the value in the active cell occurs in the range selected. If that number is greater than 1, you format the cell yellow.

```
Sub Macro1()

'Step 1: Declare your variables
  Dim MyRange As Range
  Dim MyCell As Range


'Step 2: Define the target range
  Set MyRange = Selection

'Step 3: Start looping through the range
  For Each MyCell In MyRange


'Step 4: Ensure the cell has text formatting
  If WorksheetFunction.CountIf(MyRange, MyCell.Value) > 1
          Then
  MyCell.Interior.ColorIndex = 36
  End If


'Step 5: Get the next cell in the range
  Next MyCell

End Sub
```

Step 1 declares two Range object variables. MyRange holds the entire target range, and MyCell holds each cell in the range as the macro enumerates through them one by one.

Step 2 fills the MyRange variable with the target range. In this example, you use the selected range — the range selected on the spreadsheet. You can easily set the MyRange variable to a specific range, such as Range("A1:Z100"). Also, if your target range is a named range, you could simply enter its name: Range("MyNamedRange").

Step 3 starts looping through each cell in the target range, activating each cell.

The WorksheetFunction object provides a way to run many Excel spread-sheet functions in VBA. Step 4 uses the WorksheetFunction object to run a CountIf function in VBA. In this case, you count the number of times the active cell value (MyCell.Value) is found in the given range (MyRange). If the CountIf expression evaluates to greater than 1, the macro changes the interior color of the cell.

Step 5 loops back to get the next cell. After all cells in the target range are activated, the macro ends.

How to use the macro

To implement this macro, you can copy and paste it into a standard module:

1. **Activate Visual Basic Editor by pressing Alt+F11.**
2. **Right-click the project/workbook name in the project window.**
3. **Choose Insert ⇨ Module.**
4. **Type or paste the code.**

Hiding All Rows Except Rows Containing Duplicate Data

With the preceding macro, you can quickly find and highlight duplicates in your data. This technique in itself can be quite useful. But if you have many records in your range, you may want to take the extra step of hiding all nonduplicate rows.

Look at the example in Figure 7-5. You can easily see which rows have duplicate values because they are the only rows displayed.

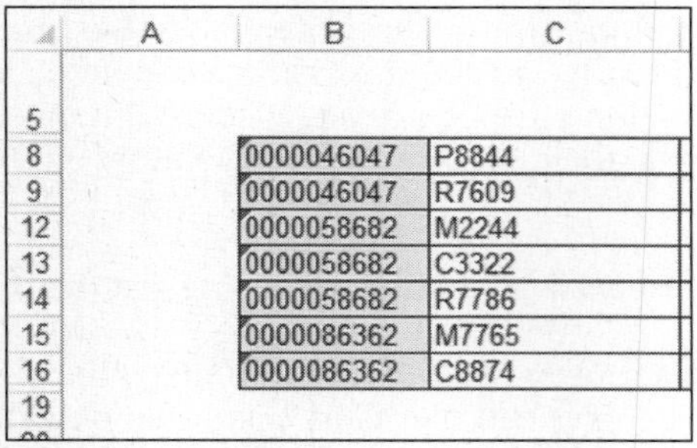

Figure 7-5:
Only rows
that contain
duplicate
values are
visible.

⊿	A	B	C	
5				
8		0000046047	P8844	
9		0000046047	R7609	
12		0000058682	M2244	
13		0000058682	C3322	
14		0000058682	R7786	
15		0000086362	M7765	
16		0000086362	C8874	
19				

How the macro works

The macro enumerates through the cells in the target range, leveraging the For Each statement to activate each cell one at a time. You then use the CountIf function to count the number of times the value in the active cell occurs in the range selected. If that number is 1, you hide the row in which the active cell resides. If that number is greater than 1, you format the cell yellow and leave the row visible.

```
Sub Macro1()

'Step 1: Declare your variables
    Dim MyRange As Range
    Dim MyCell As Range


'Step 2: Define the target range
    Set MyRange = Selection


'Step 3: Start looping through the range
    For Each MyCell In MyRange


'Step 4: Ensure the cell has text formatting
    If Not IsEmpty(MyCell) Then

        If WorksheetFunction.CountIf(MyRange, MyCell) > 1 Then
            MyCell.Interior.ColorIndex = 36
            MyCell.EntireRow.Hidden = False
        Else
            MyCell.EntireRow.Hidden = True
        End If
```

```
   End If

'Step 5: Get the next cell in the range
   Next MyCell

End Sub
```

Step 1 declares two Range object variables. MyRange holds the entire target range, and MyCell holds each cell in the range as you enumerate through them one by one.

Step 2 fills the MyRange variable with the target range. In this example, you use the selected range — the range selected on the spreadsheet. You can easily set the MyRange variable to a specific range, such as Range("A1:Z100"). Also, if your target range is a named range, you could simply enter its name: Range("MyNamedRange").

Step 3 loops through each cell in the target range, activating each cell as you go through.

In Step 4, you use the IsEmpty function to make sure that the cell is not empty. In this way, the macro won't automatically hide empty rows in the target range.

You then use the WorksheetFunction object to run a CountIf function in VBA. In this particular scenario, you count the number of times the active cell value (MyCell.Value) is found in the given range (MyRange).

If the CountIf expression evaluates to greater than 1, you change the interior color of the cell and set the EntireRow property to Hidden=False. This step ensures that the row is visible.

If the CountIf expression does not evaluate to greater than 1, the macro jumps to the Else argument. Here you set the EntireRow property to Hidden=True. This ensures the row is not visible.

Step 5 loops back to get the next cell. After all cells in the target range are activated, the macro ends.

 Because you define the target range as the current selection, you want to be sure to select the area where your data exists before running this code. You wouldn't want to select an entire column or the entire worksheet. Otherwise, any cell that contains data that is unique (not duplicated) triggers the hiding of the row. Alternatively, to ensure that this is never a problem, you can explicitly define the target range — such as Set MyRange = Range("A1:Z100").

How to use the macro

To implement this macro, you can copy and paste it into a standard module:

1. **Activate Visual Basic Editor by pressing Alt+F11.**
2. **Right-click the project/workbook name in the project window.**
3. **Choose Insert ⇨ Module.**
4. **Type or paste the code.**

Selectively Hiding AutoFilter Drop-Down Arrows

It goes without saying that the AutoFilter function in Excel is one of the most useful. Nothing else allows for faster on-the-spot filtering and analysis. The only problem is that the standard AutoFilter functionality applies drop-down arrows to every column in the chosen data set, as shown in Figure 7-6. This behavior is all right in most situations, but what if you want to prevent your users from using the AutoFilter drop-down arrows on some of the columns in your data?

Figure 7-6:
AutoFilter
adds
drop-down
arrows to all
columns in
your data.

Region	Q1	Q2	Q3	Q4	Product Number
East	771	930	0	376	M2244
East	392	9	657	39	M3345
East	0	190	557	0	M7765
East	240	499	827	135	P8895
North	908	553	924	421	P8867
North	90	201	0	645	P8844
North	565	0	596	13	C3322
South	982	885	660	437	C5521
South	87	0	478	502	C5567
South	236	800	687	0	C8874
West	0	0	172	96	R7786
West	104	886	421	56	R7609

The good news is that with a little VBA, you can selectively hide AutoFilter drop-down arrows, as shown in Figure 7-7.

Figure 7-7:
With a little
VBA, you
can hide
certain
drop-down
arrows.

Region	Q1	Q2	Q3	Q4	Product Number
East	771	930	0	376	M2244
East	392	9	657	39	M3345
East	0	190	557	0	M7765
East	240	499	827	135	P8895
North	908	553	924	421	P8867
North	90	201	0	645	P8844
North	565	0	596	13	C3322
South	982	885	660	437	C5521
South	87	0	478	502	C5567
South	236	800	687	0	C8874
West	0	0	172	96	R7786
West	104	886	421	56	R7609

How the macro works

In VBA, you can use the AutoFilter object to turn on AutoFilters for a specific range. For instance:

```
Range("B5:G5").AutoFilter
```

After an AutoFilter is applied, you can manipulate each column in the Auto Filter by pointing to it. For example, to perform some action on the third column in the AutoFilter:

```
Range("B5:G5").AutoFilter Field:3
```

You can perform many actions on an AutoFilter field. In this scenario, you are interested in making the drop-down arrow on field 3 invisible. For this, you can use the VisibleDropDown parameter. Setting this parameter to False makes the drop-down arrow invisible:

```
Range("B5:G5").AutoFilter Field:3, VisibleDropDown:=False
```

Here is an example of a macro where you turn on AutoFilters and then make only the first and last drop-down arrows visible:

```
Sub Macro1()

With Range("B5:G5")
.AutoFilter
.AutoFilter Field:=1, VisibleDropDown:=True
.AutoFilter Field:=2, VisibleDropDown:=False
.AutoFilter Field:=3, VisibleDropDown:=False
.AutoFilter Field:=4, VisibleDropDown:=False
.AutoFilter Field:=5, VisibleDropDown:=False
.AutoFilter Field:=6, VisibleDropDown:=True
End With

End Sub
```

You are not only pointing to a specific range but also explicitly pointing to each field. When implementing this type of macro in your environment, alter the code to suit your particular data set.

How to use the macro

To implement this macro, you can copy and paste it into a standard module:

1. **Activate Visual Basic Editor by pressing Alt+F11.**
2. **Right-click the project/workbook name in the project window.**
3. **Choose Insert⇨Module.**
4. **Type or paste the code.**

Copying Filtered Rows to a New Workbook

Often, when you're working with a set of data that is AutoFiltered, you want to extract the filtered rows to a new workbook. Of course, you can manually copy the filtered rows, open a new workbook, paste the rows, and then format the newly pasted data so that all the columns fit. But if you are doing this sequence frequently enough, you may want to use a macro to speed up the process.

How the macro works

The following macro captures the AutoFilter range, opens a new workbook, and then pastes the data:

```
Sub Macro1()

'Step 1: Check for AutoFilter and exit if none exists
    If ActiveSheet.AutoFilterMode = False Then
    Exit Sub
    End If

'Step 2: Copy the autofiltered range to new workbook
    ActiveSheet.AutoFilter.Range.Copy
    Workbooks.Add.Worksheets(1).Paste
```

```
'Step 3: Size the columns to fit
   Cells.EntireColumn.AutoFit

End Sub
```

Step 1 uses the AutoFilterMode property to check whether the sheet has AutoFilters applied. If not, you exit the procedure.

Each AutoFilter object has a Range property. This Range property obligingly returns the rows to which the AutoFilter applies, meaning it returns only the rows that are shown in the filtered data set. In Step 2, you use the Copy method to capture those rows, and then you paste the rows to a new workbook. Note that you use Workbooks.Add.Worksheets(1), which tells Excel to paste the data into the first sheet of the newly created workbook.

Step 3 simply tells Excel to size the column widths to autofit the data you just pasted.

How to use the macro

To implement this macro, you can copy and paste it into a standard module:

1. **Activate Visual Basic Editor by pressing Alt+F11.**
2. **Right-click the project/workbook name in the project window.**
3. **Choose Insert ⇨ Module.**
4. **Type or paste the code.**

Displaying Filtered Columns in the Status Bar

When you have a large table with many columns that are AutoFiltered, know which columns are filtered and which aren't can be difficult. You could scroll through the columns, peering at each AutoFilter drop-down list for the tell-tale icon indicating that the column is filtered, but that can get old quickly.

The macro in this section helps by specifically listing in the status bar all filtered columns. The status bar runs across the bottom of the Excel window, as shown in Figure 7-8.

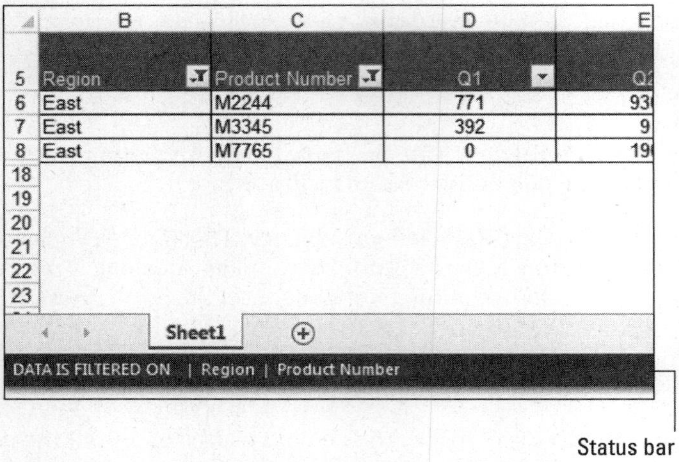

▲	B	C	D	E
5	Region ▼	Product Number ▼	Q1 ▼	Q2
6	East	M2244	771	93(
7	East	M3345	392	9
8	East	M7765	0	19(
18				
19				
20				
21				
22				
23				

◄ ► **Sheet1** ⊕

DATA IS FILTERED ON | Region | Product Number

Status bar

Figure 7-8:
All filtered columns are listed in the status bar.

How the macro works

The macro loops through the fields in your AutoFiltered data set. As you loop, you check to see if each field is filtered. If so, you capture the field name in a text string. After looping through all the fields, you pass the final string to the StatusBar property:

```
Sub Macro1()


'Step 1: Declare your variables
  Dim AF As AutoFilter
  Dim TargetField As String
  Dim strOutput As String
  Dim i As Integer


'Step 2: Check if AutoFilter exists - if not, exit
  If ActiveSheet.AutoFilterMode = False Then
    Application.StatusBar = False
    Exit Sub
  End If


'Step 3: Set AutoFilter and start looping
  Set AF = ActiveSheet.AutoFilter
  For i = 1 To AF.Filters.Count
```

```
'Step 4: Capture filtered field names
 If AF.Filters(i).On Then
  TargetField = AF.Range.Cells(1, i).Value
 strOutput = strOutput & " | " & TargetField
 End If
 Next


'Step 5: Display the filters if there are any
 If strOutput = "" Then
 Application.StatusBar = False
 Else
 Application.StatusBar = "DATA IS FILTERED ON " &
         strOutput
 End If

End Sub
```

Step 1 declares four variables. AF is an AutoFilter variable that manipulates
the AutoFilter object. TargetField is a String variable that holds the field
names of any filtered field. strOutput is the String variable you use to build
out the final text that appears into the status bar. Finally, the i variable
serves as a simple counter, allowing you to iterate through the fields in your
AutoFilter.

Step 2 checks the AutoFilterMode property to see if a sheet even has
AutoFilters applied. If not, you set the StatusBar property to False, which has
the effect of clearing the status bar, releasing control back to Excel. You then
exit the procedure.

Step 3 sets the AF variable to the AutoFilter on the active sheet. You then
set your counter to count from 1 to the maximum number of columns in the
AutoFiltered range. The AutoFilter object keeps track of its columns with
index numbers. Column 1 is index 1; column 2 is index 2, and so on. The idea
is that you can loop through each column in the AutoFilter by using the i variable as the index number.

Step 4 checks the status of AF.Filters object for each (i), where i is the index
number of the column you're evaluating. If the AutoFilter for that column is
filtered in any way, the status for that column is On.

If the filter for the column is on, you capture the name of the field in the
TargetField variable. You actually get the name of the field by referencing
the Range of your AF AutoFilter object. With this range, you can use the Cells
item to pinpoint the field name. Cells(1,1) captures the value in row one,
column one. Cells(1,2) captures the value in row one, column two, and so on.

As you can see in Step 4, you've hard-coded the row to 1 and used the i variable to indicate the column index. As the macro iterates through the columns, it always captures the value in row one as the TargetField name (row one is where the field name is likely to be).

After you have the TargetField name, you can pass that information to a simple string container (strOutput in your case). strOutput keeps all target field names you find and concatenates them into a readable text string.

Step 5 first checks to make sure that something is in the strOutput string. If strOutput is empty, the macro did not find any filtered columns in your AutoFilter . In this case, Step 5 simply sets the StatusBar property to False, releasing control back to Excel.

If strOutput is not empty, Step 5 sets the StatusBar property to equal some helper text along with your strOutput string.

How to use the macro

You ideally want this macro to run each time a field is filtered. However, Excel does not have an OnAutoFilter event. The closest thing to that event is the Worksheet_Calculate event. That being said, AutoFilters in themselves don't calculate anything, so you need to enter a volatile function on the sheet that contains your AutoFiltered data. A *volatile function* forces a recalculation when any change is made on the worksheet.

In the sample files that come with this book, note that you use the Now function. The Now function is a volatile function that returns a date and time. With this function on the sheet, the worksheet is sure to recalculate each time the AutoFilter is changed.

Place the Now function anywhere on your sheet by typing =Now() in any cell. Then copy and paste the macro in the Worksheet_Calculate event code window as follows:

1. **Activate Visual Basic Editor by pressing Alt+F11.**

2. **In the project window, find your project/workbook name and click the plus sign next to it in order to see all the sheets.**

3. **Click the sheet from which you want to trigger the code.**

4. **Select the Calculate event from the Event drop-down list, as shown in Figure 7-9.**

5. **Type or paste the code.**

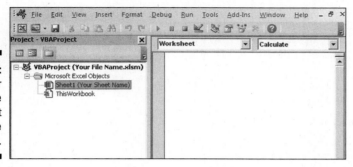

Figure 7-9:
Enter your
code in the
Worksheet
Calculate
event.

To make the code run as smoothly as possible, consider adding the following two pieces of code under the worksheet calculate event:

```
Private Sub Worksheet_Deactivate()

Application.StatusBar = False

End Sub

Private Sub Worksheet_Activate()

Call Worksheet_Calculate

End Sub
```

Also, add this piece of code in the workbook BeforeClose event:

```
Private Sub Workbook_BeforeClose(Cancel As Boolean)

Application.StatusBar = False

End Sub
```

The Worksheet_Deactivate event clears the status bar when you move to another sheet or workbook, avoiding confusion as you move between sheets.

The Worksheet_Activate event fires the macro in Worksheet_Calculate. This event brings back the status bar indicators when you navigate back to the filtered sheet.

The Workbook_BeforeClose event clears the status bar when you close the workbook, avoiding confusion as you move between workbooks.

Part IV
Macro-Charging Reports and Emails

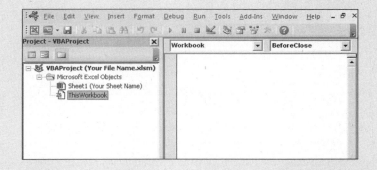

Visit www.dummies.com/extras/excelmacros to discover how to send Excel reporting data directly to PowerPoint by using VBA.

In this part . . .

- ✔ Gain an understanding of how macros can be leveraged to automate your reporting processes.

- ✔ Discover how to automate the more mundane aspects of building pivot tables.

- ✔ See how macros can help work with the charts in your reports and dashboards.

- ✔ Explore some of the techniques you can leverage to send emails from Excel.

Chapter 8

Automating Common Reporting Tasks

For those of us tasked with building dashboards and reports, PivotTables and charts are a daily part of our work life. Few of us have had the inclination to automate any aspect of these reporting tools with macros. But some aspects of our work lend themselves to a bit of automation. In this chapter, you explore a handful of macros that can help you save time and gain efficiencies when working with pivot tables and charts.

Refreshing All Pivot Tables in a Workbook

It's not uncommon to have multiple pivot tables in the same workbook. Many times, these pivot tables link to data that changes, requiring a refresh of the pivot tables. If you find that you need to refresh your pivot tables en masse, you can use the macro in this section.

How the macro works

It's important to know that each PivotTable object is a child of the worksheet it sits in. The macro has to loop through the worksheets in a workbook first, and then loop through the pivot tables in each worksheet. This macro does just that — loops through the worksheets, and then loops through the pivot tables. During each loop, the macro refreshes the pivot table.

```
Sub Macro1()

'Step 1: Declare your variables
    Dim ws As Worksheet
    Dim pt As PivotTable


'Step 2: Loop through each sheet in workbook
    For Each ws In ThisWorkbook.Worksheets


'Step 3: Loop through each pivot table
        For Each pt In ws.PivotTables
            pt.RefreshTable
        Next pt
    Next ws

End Sub
```

Step 1 first declares an object called ws. This step creates a memory container for each worksheet you loop through. It also declares an object called pt, which holds each pivot table the macro loops through.

Step 2 starts the looping, telling Excel you want to evaluate all worksheets in this workbook. Note that you're using ThisWorkbook instead of ActiveWorkbook. The ThisWorkbook object refers to the workbook that contains the code. The ActiveWorkbook object refers to the currently active workbook. They often return the same object, but if the workbook running the code is not the active workbook, they return different objects. In this case, you don't want to risk refreshing pivot tables in other workbooks, so you use ThisWorkbook.

Step 3 loops through all pivot tables in each worksheet, and then triggers the RefreshTable method. After all pivot tables have been refreshed, you move to the next sheet. After all sheets have been evaluated, the macro ends.

As an alternative method for refreshing all pivot tables in the workbook, you can use ThisWorkbook.RefreshAll. This method refreshes all pivot tables in the workbook — but it also refreshes all query tables. If you have data tables that are connected to an external source or the web, they will be affected by the RefreshAll method. If this is not a concern, you can simply enter ThisWorkbook.RefreshAll into a standard module.

How to use the macro

To implement this macro, you can copy and paste it into a standard module:

1. **Activate Visual Basic Editor by pressing Alt+F11.**
2. **Right-click the project/workbook name in the project window.**
3. **Choose Insert ⇨ Module.**
4. **Type or paste the code.**

Creating a Pivot Table Inventory Summary

When your workbook contains multiple pivot tables, it's often helpful to have an inventory summary that outlines basic details about the pivot tables (similar to the one in Figure 8-1).

Figure 8-1: A pivot table inventory summary.

	A	B	C	D	E	F
1	Pivot Name	Worksheet	Location	Cache Index	Source Data Location	Row Count
2	PivotTable10	Product Categories	$A$3:$I$11	2	Raw Data'!$A$3:$N$59469	59466
3	PivotTable9	Internet Sales	$A$3:$D$11	3	Raw Data'!$A$3:$N$59468	59465
4	PivotTable11	Units Sold	$A$3:$I$11	1	Raw Data'!$A$3:$N$59470	59467
5	PivotTable12	Sales by Year	$A$3:$I$45	2	Raw Data'!$A$3:$N$59469	59466
6						

With this type of summary, you can quickly see important information such as the location of each pivot table, the location of each pivot table's source data, and the pivot cache index that each pivot table is using.

The macro in this section outputs such a summary.

How the macro works

When you create a PivotTable Object variable, you expose the pivot table's properties, such as its name, location, and cache index. In this macro, you loop through each pivot table in the workbook and extract specific properties into a new worksheet.

Because each PivotTable object is a child of the worksheet it sits in, you have to first loop through the worksheets in a workbook, and then loop through the pivot tables in each worksheet.

Take a moment to walk through the steps of this macro in detail:

```
Sub Macro1()

'Step 1:  Declare your variables
    Dim ws As Worksheet
    Dim pt As PivotTable
    Dim MyCell As Range


'Step 2: Add a new sheet with column headers
    Worksheets.Add
    Range("A1:F1") = Array("Pivot Name", "Worksheet", _
                        "Location", "Cache Index", _
                        "Source Data Location", _
                        "Row Count")


'Step 3:  Start cursor at cell A2 setting the anchor here
    Set MyCell = ActiveSheet.Range("A2")


'Step 4: Loop through each sheet in workbook
    For Each ws In Worksheets


'Step 5: Loop through each pivot table
        For Each pt In ws.PivotTables
        MyCell.Offset(0, 0) = pt.Name
        MyCell.Offset(0, 1) = pt.Parent.Name
        MyRange.Offset(0, 2) = pt.TableRange2.Address
        MyRange.Offset(0, 3) = pt.CacheIndex
        MyRange.Offset(0, 4) = Application.ConvertFormula _
        (pt.PivotCache.SourceData, xlR1C1, xlA1)
        MyRange.Offset(0, 5) = pt.PivotCache.RecordCount


'Step 6:  Move cursor down one row and set a new anchor
        Set MyRange = MyRange.Offset(1, 0)


'Step 7:  Work through all pivot tables and worksheets
        Next pt
    Next ws
```

```
'Step 8: Size columns to fit
    ActiveSheet.Cells.EntireColumn.AutoFit

End Sub
```

Step 1 declares an object called ws. This step creates a memory container for each worksheet you loop through. You then declare an object called pt, which holds each pivot table you loop through. Finally, you create a range variable called MyCell, which acts as your cursor as you fill in the inventory summary.

Step 2 creates a new worksheet and adds column headings that range from A1 to F1. Note that you can add column heading using a simple array that contains your header labels. This new worksheet remains your active sheet from here on out.

Just as you would manually place your cursor into a cell if you were to start typing data, Step 3 places the MyCell cursor in cell A2 of the active sheet. This step establishes your anchor point, allowing you to navigate from here.

Throughout the macro, you see the use of the Offset property. The Offset property allows you to move a cursor *x* rows and *x* columns from an anchor point. For instance, Range(A2).Offset(0,1) would move the cursor one column to the right. If you wanted to move the cursor one row down, you would enter Range(A2).Offset(1, 0).

In the macro, you navigate by using Offset on MyCell. For example, MyCell. Offset(0,4) would move the cursor four columns to the right of the anchor cell. After the cursor is in place, you can enter data.

Step 4 starts the looping, telling Excel you want to evaluate all worksheets in this workbook.

Step 5 loops through all pivot tables in each worksheet. For each pivot table found, it extracts the appropriate property and fills in the table based on the cursor position (see Step 3).

You are using six pivot table properties: Name, Parent.Range, TableRange2. Address, CacheIndex, PivotCache.SourceData, and PivotCache.Recordcount. The Name property returns the name of the pivot table. The Parent.Range property gives you the sheet where the pivot table resides. The TableRange2. Address property returns the range that the PivotTable object sits in.

The CacheIndex property returns the index number of the pivot cache for the pivot table. A *pivot cache* is a memory container that stores all the data for a pivot table. When you create a new pivot table, Excel takes a snapshot of the source data and creates a pivot cache. Each time you refresh a pivot table, Excel goes back to the source data and takes another snapshot, thereby refreshing the pivot cache. Each pivot cache has a SourceData property that identifies the location of the data used to create the pivot cache. The PivotCache.SourceData property tells us which range will be called on when you refresh the pivot table. You can also pull out the record count of the source data by using the PivotCache.Recordcount property.

In Step 6, each time the macro encounters a new pivot table, it moves the MyCell cursor down a row, effectively starting a new row for each pivot table.

Step 7 tells Excel to loop back to iterate through all pivot tables and all worksheets. After all pivot tables have been evaluated, you move to the next sheet. After all sheets have been evaluated, the macro moves to the last step.

Step 8 finishes with a little formatting, sizing the columns to fit the data.

How to use the macro

To implement this macro, you can copy and paste it into a standard module:

1. **Activate Visual Basic Editor by pressing Alt+F11.**
2. **Right-click the project/workbook name in the project window.**
3. **Choose Insert ⇨ Module.**
4. **Type or paste the code.**

Adjusting All Pivot Data Field Titles

When you create a pivot table, Excel tries to help you out by prefacing each data field header with *Sum of, Count of,* or whichever operation you use. Often, this behavior is not conducive to your reporting needs. You want clean titles that match your data source as closely as possible. Although it's true that you can manually adjust the titles for data fields (one at a time), the following macro fixes them all in one go.

How the macro works

Ideally, the name of the each data item matches the field name from your source data set (the original source data used to create the pivot table).

Unfortunately, pivot tables won't allow you to name a data field with the same name as the source data field. The workaround for this limitation is to add a space to the end of the field name. Excel considers the field name (with a space) to be different from the source data field name. And the readers of your spreadsheet don't notice the space after the name.

The macro utilizes this workaround to rename your data fields. It loops through each data field in the pivot table, and then resets each header to match its respective field in the source data plus a space character.

```
Sub Macro1()

'Step 1: Declare your variables
    Dim pt As PivotTable
    Dim pf As PivotField


'Step 2: Point to the pivot table in the active cell
    On Error Resume Next
    Set pt = ActiveSheet.PivotTables(ActiveCell.
        PivotTable.Name)


'Step 3:  Exit if active cell is not in a pivot table
    If pt Is Nothing Then
    MsgBox "You must place your cursor inside a pivot
        table."
    Exit Sub
    End If


'Step 4:  Loop through all pivot fields and adjust titles
    For Each pf In pt.DataFields
        pf.Caption = pf.SourceName & Chr(160)
    Next pf

End Sub
```

Step 1 declares two object variables. It uses pt as the memory container for your pivot table, and pf as a memory container for the data fields. This step allows the macro to loop through all the data fields in the pivot table.

The macro is designed so that you infer the active pivot table based on the active cell. In other words, the active cell must be inside a pivot table for this macro to run. The assumption is that when the cursor is inside a particular pivot table, you want to perform the macro action on that pivot table.

Step 2 sets the pt variable to the name of the pivot table on which the active cell is found. You do this by using the ActiveCell.PivotTable.Name property to get the name of the target pivot.

If the active cell is not inside a pivot table, an error is thrown. For this reason, you use the On Error Resume Next statement to tell Excel to continue with the macro if there is an error.

In Step 3, you check to see whether the pt variable is filled with a PivotTable object. If the pt variable is set to Nothing, the active cell was not on a pivot table, thus no pivot table could be assigned to the variable. If this is the case, you use a message box to tell the user, and then you exit the procedure.

If the macro reaches Step 4, it has successfully pointed to a pivot table. The macro uses a For Each statement to iterate through each data field. Each time a new pivot field is selected, the macro changes the field name by setting the Caption property to match the field's SourceName. The SourceName property returns the name of the matching field in the original source data.

To that name, the macro concatenates a nonbreaking space character: Chr(160).

Every character has an underlying ASCII code, similar to a serial number. For instance, the lowercase letter *a* has an ASCII code of 97. The lowercase letter *c* has an ASCII code of 99. Likewise, invisible characters such as the space have a code. You can use invisible characters in your macro by passing their code through the CHR function.

After the name has been changed, the macro moves to the next data field. After all the data fields have been evaluated, the macro ends.

How to use the macro

To implement this macro, you can copy and paste it into a standard module:

1. **Activate Visual Basic Editor by pressing Alt+F11.**

2. **Right-click the project/workbook name in the project window.**

3. **Choose Insert ⇨ Module.**

4. **Type or paste the code.**

Setting All Data Items to Sum

When creating a pivot table, Excel defaults to summarizing your data by either counting or summing the items. The logic Excel uses to decide whether to sum or count the fields you add to your pivot table is simple. If all cells in a column contain numeric data, Excel chooses Sum. If the field you are adding contains a blank or text, Excel chooses Count.

Although this logic seems to make sense, in many instances a pivot field that should be summed legitimately contains blanks. In these cases, you are forced to manually go in after Excel and change the calculation type from Count to Sum. That's if you're paying attention! It's not uncommon to miss the fact that a pivot field is being counted instead of summed.

The macro in this section aims to help by automatically setting each data item's calculation type to Sum.

How the macro works

This macro loops through each data field in the pivot table and changes the Function property to xlSum. You can alter this macro to use any calculation choice: xlCount, xlAverage, xlMin, xlMax, and so on. When you go into the code window and type pf.Function =, you see a drop-down list with your choices, as shown in Figure 8-2.

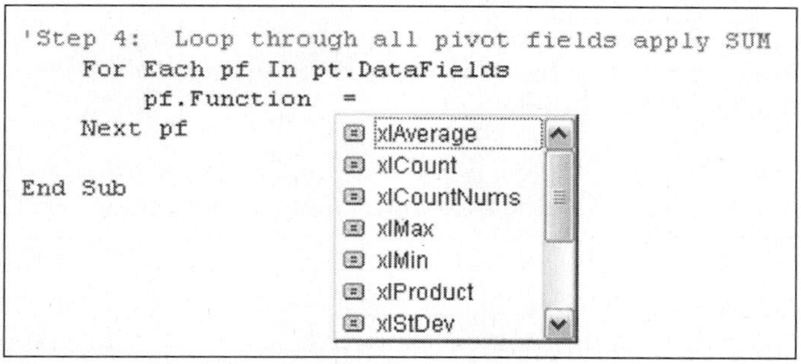

Figure 8-2: Excel displays your enumeration choices.

```
'Step 4:  Loop through all pivot fields apply SUM
    For Each pf In pt.DataFields
        pf.Function =
    Next pf

End Sub
```

xlAverage
xlCount
xlCountNums
xlMax
xlMin
xlProduct
xlStDev

```
Sub Macro1()

'Step 1: Declare your variables
    Dim pt As PivotTable
    Dim pf As PivotField


'Step 2: Point to the pivot table in the active cell
    On Error Resume Next
    Set pt = ActiveSheet.PivotTables(ActiveCell.
        PivotTable.Name)
```

```
'Step 3:  Exit if active cell is not in a pivot table
    If pt Is Nothing Then
    MsgBox "You must place your cursor inside a pivot
        table."
    Exit Sub
    End If


'Step 4:  Loop through all pivot fields and apply SUM
    For Each pf In pt.DataFields
        pf.Function = xlSum
    Next pf

End Sub
```

Step 1 declares two object variables. It uses pt as the memory container for the pivot table and pf as a memory container for the data fields. This step allows you to loop through all the data fields in the pivot table.

This macro is designed so that you infer the active pivot table based on the active cell. The active cell must be inside a pivot table for this macro to run. The assumption is that when the cursor is inside a particular pivot table, you want to perform the macro action on that pivot.

Step 2 sets the pt variable to the name of the pivot table on which the active cell is found. You do this by using the ActiveCell.PivotTable.Name property to get the name of the target pivot.

If the active cell is not inside a pivot table, an error is thrown. For this reason, you use the On Error Resume Next statement to tell Excel to continue with the macro if there is an error.

Step 3 checks to see whether the pt variable is filled with a PivotTable object. If the pt variable is set to Nothing, the active cell was not on a pivot table, thus no pivot table could be assigned to the variable. If this is the case, you use a message box to tell the user, and then you exit the procedure.

If the macro has reached Step 4, it has successfully pointed to a pivot table. It uses a For Each statement to iterate through each data field. Each time a new pivot field is selected, the macro alters the Function property to set the calculation used by the field. In this case, you're setting all the data fields in the pivot table to Sum.

After the function has been changed, you move to the next data field. After all the data fields have been evaluated, the macro ends.

How to use the macro

To implement this macro, you can copy and paste it into a standard module:

1. **Activate Visual Basic Editor by pressing Alt+F11.**
2. **Right-click the project/workbook name in the project window.**
3. **Choose Insert ➪ Module.**
4. **Type or paste the code.**

Applying Number Formatting to All Data Items

A pivot table does not inherently store number formatting in its pivot cache because formatting takes up memory. To be as lean as possible, the pivot cache contains only data. Unfortunately, as a result, you need to apply number formatting to every field you add to a pivot table. This process takes from 8 to 10 mouse clicks for every data field you add. When you have pivot tables that contain five or more data fields, you're talking about more than 40 mouse clicks!

Ideally, a pivot table should be able to look back at its source data and adopt the number formatting from the fields there. The macro outlined in this section is designed to do just that. It recognizes the number formatting in the pivot table's source data and applies the appropriate formatting to each field automatically.

How the macro works

Before running this code, you want to make sure that

- ✔ **The source data for your pivot table is accessible.** The macro needs to see it to capture the correct number formatting.

- ✔ **The source data is appropriately formatted.** Money fields are formatted as currency, value fields are formatted as numbers, and so on.

This macro uses the PivotTable SourceData property to find the location of the source data. It then loops through each column in the source, capturing the header name and the number format of the first value under each column. After it has that information, the macro determines whether any data fields match the evaluated column. If it finds a match, the number formatting is applied to that data field.

```
Sub Macro1()

'Step 1: Declare your variables
    Dim pt As PivotTable
    Dim pf As PivotField
    Dim SrcRange As Range
    Dim strFormat As String
    Dim strLabel As String
    Dim i As Integer


'Step 2: Point to the pivot table in the active cell
    On Error Resume Next
    Set pt = ActiveSheet.PivotTables(ActiveCell.
        PivotTable.Name)


'Step 3:  Exit if active cell is not in a pivot table
    If pt Is Nothing Then
    MsgBox "You must place your cursor inside a pivot
        table."
    Exit Sub
    End If


'Step 4: Capture the source range
    Set SrcRange = _
    Range(Application.ConvertFormula(pt.SourceData,
        xlR1C1, xlA1))


'Step 5: Start looping through the columns in source range
    For i = 1 To SrcRange.Columns.Count


'Step 6: Trap the source column name and number format
        strLabel = SrcRange.Cells(1, i).Value
        strFormat = SrcRange.Cells(2, i).NumberFormat


'Step 7: Loop through fields in the pivot table data area
        For Each pf In pt.DataFields
```

```
'Step 8: Check for match on SourceName then apply format
            If pf.SourceName = strLabel Then
            pf.NumberFormat = strFormat
            End If
        Next pf
    Next i

End Sub
```

Step 1 declares six variables. It uses pt as the memory container for your pivot table and pf as a memory container for your data fields. The SrcRange variable holds the data range for the source data. The strFormat and strLabel variables are both text string variables used to hold the source column label and number formatting, respectively. The i variable serves as a counter, helping you enumerate through the columns of the source data range.

The active cell must be inside a pivot table for this macro to run. The assumption is that when the cursor is inside a particular pivot table, you want to perform the macro action on that pivot.

Step 2 sets the pt variable to the name of the pivot table on which the active cell is found. You do this by using the ActiveCell.PivotTable.Name property to get the name of the target pivot.

If the active cell is not inside a pivot table, an error is thrown. For this reason, the macro uses the On Error Resume Next statement to tell Excel to continue with the macro if there is an error.

Step 3 checks to see whether the pt variable is filled with a PivotTable object. If the pt variable is set to Nothing, the active cell was not on a pivot table, thus no pivot table could be assigned to the variable. If this is the case, you use a message box to tell the user, and then you exit the procedure.

If the macro reaches Step 4, it has successfully pointed to a pivot table. You immediately fill your SrcRange Object variable with the pivot table's source data range.

All pivot tables have a SourceData property that points to the address of its source. Unfortunately, the address is stored in the R1C1 reference style, like this: 'Raw Data'!R3C1:R59470C14. Range objects cannot use the R1C1 style, so you need to convert the address to 'Raw Data'!$A$3:$N$59470.

The fix is simple. You simply pass the SourceData property through the Application.ConvertFormula function, which converts ranges to and from the R1C1 reference style.

After the range is captured, the macro starts looping through the columns in the source range. In this case, you manage the looping by using the i integer as an index number for the columns in the source range. You start the index number at 1 and end it at the maximum number of rows in the source range.

As the macro loops through the columns in the source range, you capture the column header label and the column format. You do this action with the aid of the Cells item. The Cells item gives you a handy way of selecting ranges through code. It requires only relative row and column positions as parameters. Cells(1,1) translates to row 1, column 1 (or the header row of the first column). Cells(2, 1) translates to row 2, column 1 (or the first value in the first column).

strLabel is filled by the header label taken from row 1 of the selected column. strFormat is filled with the number formatting from row 2 of the selected column that is selected.

At this point, the macro has connected with the pivot table's source data and captured the first column name and number formatting for that column. In Step 7, it starts looping through the data fields in the pivot table.

Step 8 simply compares each data field to see whether its source matches the name in strLabel. If it does, this step will set the number formatting of the pivot field to the same format as the source data field.

After all data fields have been evaluated, the macro increments i to the next column in the source range. After all columns have been evaluated, the macro ends.

How to use the macro

To implement this macro, you can copy and paste it into a standard module:

1. **Activate Visual Basic Editor by pressing Alt+F11.**
2. **Right-click project/workbook name in the project window.**
3. **Choose Insert ⇨ Module.**
4. **Type or paste the code.**

Sorting All Fields in Alphabetical Order

If you frequently add data to your pivot tables, you may notice that new data doesn't automatically fall into the sort order of the existing pivot data. Instead, it gets tacked to the bottom of the existing data. This means your drop-down lists display existing data sorted alphabetically but display new data at the bottom of the list.

How the macro works

The macro in this section resets the sorting on all data fields, ensuring that any new data snaps into place. You should run the macro each time you refresh your pivot table. In the code, you enumerate through each data field in the pivot table, sorting each one as you go.

```
Sub Macro1()

'Step 1: Declare your variables
    Dim pt As PivotTable
    Dim pf As PivotField


'Step 2: Point to the pivot table in the active cell
    On Error Resume Next
    Set pt = ActiveSheet.PivotTables(ActiveCell.
        PivotTable.Name)


'Step 3:  Exit if active cell is not in a pivot table
    If pt Is Nothing Then
    MsgBox "You must place your cursor inside a pivot
        table."
    Exit Sub
    End If


'Step 4:  Loop through all pivot fields and sort
    For Each pf In pt.PivotFields
        pf.AutoSort xlAscending, pf.Name
    Next pf

End Sub
```

Step 1 declares two object variables: pt is the memory container for the pivot table and pf is the memory container for your data fields. This step allows the macro to loop through all the data fields in the pivot table.

The active cell must be inside a pivot table for the macro to run. The assumption is that when the cursor is inside a particular pivot table, you want to perform the macro action on that pivot.

In Step 2, you set the pt variable to the name of the pivot table on which the active cell is found. You do this by using the ActiveCell.PivotTable.Name property to get the name of the target pivot.

If the active cell is not inside a pivot table, an error is thrown. For this reason, you use the On Error Resume Next statement to tell Excel to continue with the macro if there is an error.

Step 3 checks to see whether the pt variable is filled with a PivotTable object. If the pt variable is set to Nothing, the active cell was not on a pivot table, thus no pivot table could be assigned to the variable. If this is the case, the macro displays a message box to notify the user and then exits the procedure.

Finally, in Step 4, you use a For Each statement to iterate through each pivot field. Each time a new pivot field is selected, you use the AutoSort method to reset the automatic sorting rules for the field. In this case, you're sorting all fields in ascending order. After all the data fields have been evaluated, the macro ends.

How to use the macro

To implement this macro, you can copy and paste it into a standard module:

1. **Activate Visual Basic Editor by pressing Alt+F11.**
2. **Right-click the project/workbook name in the project window.**
3. **Choose Insert ⇨ Module.**
4. **Type or paste the code.**

Applying Custom Sort to Data Items

On occasion, you may need to apply a custom sort to the data items in your pivot table. For instance, if you work for a company in California, your organization may want the West region to come before the North and South. In these types of situations, neither the standard ascending nor the standard descending sort order will work.

How the macro works

You can automate the custom sorting of your fields by using the Position property of the PivotItems object. With the Position property, you can assign a position number that specifies the order in which you would like see each pivot item.

In this example code, you first point to the Region pivot field in the Pvt1 PivotTable. Then you list each item along with the position number indicating the customer sort order you need:

```
Sub Macro1()

With Sheets("Sheet1").PivotTables("Pvt1").PivotFields _
    ("Region ")
    .PivotItems("West").Position = 1
    .PivotItems("North").Position = 2
    .PivotItems("South").Position = 3

End With

End Sub
```

The other solution is to set up a *custom sort list,* which is a defined list that is stored in your instance of Excel. To create a custom sort list, choose File ⇨ Options ⇨ Advanced, and then click the Edit Custom Lists button. Here, you can type West, North, South in the List Entries box and choose the Add button. After setting up a custom list, Excel will realize that the Region data items in your PivotTable match a custom list and will sort the field to match your custom list.

As brilliant as this option is, custom lists do not travel with your workbook. So a macro helps when it's impractical to expect your clients or team members to set up their own custom sort lists.

How to use the macro

You can implement this kind of a macro in a standard module:

1. **Activate Visual Basic Editor by pressing Alt+F11.**
2. **Right-click the project/workbook name in the project window.**
3. **Choose Insert ⇨ Module.**
4. **Type or paste the code.**

Applying Pivot Table Restrictions

When you send pivot table reports to clients, coworkers, managers, and other groups of people, you might want to restrict the types of actions your users can take on the reports. The macro outlined in this section demonstrates some of the protection settings available through VBA.

How the macro works

The PivotTable object exposes several properties that allow you (the developer) to restrict different features and components of a pivot table:

- **EnableWizard:** Setting this property to False disables the pivot table Tools context menu that normally activates when clicking inside a pivot table.

- **EnableDrilldown:** Setting this property to False prevents users from getting to detailed data by double-clicking a data field.

- **EnableFieldList:** Setting this property to False prevents users from activating the field list or moving pivot fields around.

- **EnableFieldDialog:** Setting this property to False disables the users' ability to alter the pivot field through the Value Field Settings dialog box.

- **PivotCache.EnableRefresh:** Setting this property to False disables the ability to refresh the pivot table.

You can set any or all these properties independently to True or False. In this macro, you apply all the restrictions to the target pivot table.

```
Sub Macro1()

'Step 1: Declare your variables
    Dim pt As PivotTable


'Step 2: Point to the pivot table in the active cell
    On Error Resume Next
    Set pt = ActiveSheet.PivotTables(ActiveCell.
        PivotTable.Name)


'Step 3:  Exit if active cell is not in a pivot table
    If pt Is Nothing Then
    MsgBox "You must place your cursor inside a pivot
        table."
    Exit Sub
    End If


'Step 4:  Apply pivot table restrictions
    With pt
        .EnableWizard = False
        .EnableDrilldown = False
        .EnableFieldList = False
        .EnableFieldDialog = False
        .PivotCache.EnableRefresh = False
    End With

End Sub
```

Step 1 declares the pt PivotTable Object variable that serves as the memory container for your pivot table.

Step 2 sets the pt variable to the name of the pivot table in which the active cell is found. You do this by using the ActiveCell.PivotTable.Name property to get the name of the target pivot.

Step 3 checks to see whether the pt variable is filled with a PivotTable object. If the pt variable is set to Nothing, the active cell was not on a pivot table, thus no pivot table could be assigned to the variable. If this is the case, you use a message box to tell the user, and then you exit the procedure.

In the last step of the macro, you are applying all pivot table restrictions.

How to use the macro

You can implement this kind of a macro in a standard module:

1. **Activate Visual Basic Editor by pressing Alt+F11.**
2. **Right-click the project/workbook name in the project window.**
3. **Choose Insert ⇨ Module.**
4. **Type or paste the code.**

Applying Pivot Field Restrictions

Like pivot table restrictions, pivot field restrictions enable you to restrict the types of actions your users can take on the pivot fields in a pivot table. The macro outlined in this section demonstrates some of the protection settings available through VBA.

How the macro works

The PivotField object exposes several properties that allow you (the developer) to restrict different features and components of a pivot table:

✔ **DragToPage:** Setting this property to False prevents users from dragging any pivot field into the Report Filter area of the pivot table.

✔ **DragToRow:** Setting this property to False prevents users from dragging any pivot field into the Row area of the pivot table.

✔ **DragToColumn:** Setting this property to False prevents users from dragging any pivot field into the Column area of the pivot table.

✔ **DragToData:** Setting this property to False prevents users from dragging any pivot field into the Data area of the pivot table.

✔ **DragToHide:** Setting this property to False prevents users from dragging pivot fields off the pivot table. It also prevents the use of the right-click menu to hide or remove pivot fields.

✔ **EnableItemSelection:** Setting this property to False disables the drop-down lists on each pivot field.

You can set any or all these properties independently to True or False. In this macro, you apply all the restrictions to the target pivot table.

```
Sub Macro1()

'Step 1: Declare your variables
    Dim pt As PivotTable
    Dim pf As PivotField


'Step 2: Point to the pivot table in the active cell
    On Error Resume Next
    Set pt = ActiveSheet.PivotTables(ActiveCell.
        PivotTable.Name)


'Step 3:  Exit if active cell is not in a pivot table
    If pt Is Nothing Then
    MsgBox "You must place your cursor inside a pivot
        table."
    Exit Sub
    End If


'Step 4:  Apply pivot field restrictions
    For Each pf In pt.PivotFields
        pf.EnableItemSelection = False
        pf.DragToPage = False
        pf.DragToRow = False
        pf.DragToColumn = False
        pf.DragToData = False
        pf.DragToHide = False
    Next pf

End Sub
```

Step 1 declares two object variables: pt is the memory container for your pivot table and pf is the memory container for your pivot fields. This step allows us to loop through all the pivot fields in the pivot table.

Set the pt variable to name of the pivot table on which the active cell is found by using the ActiveCell.PivotTable.Name property to get the name of the target pivot.

Step 3 checks to see whether the pt variable is filled with a PivotTable object. If the pt variable is set to Nothing, the active cell was not in a pivot table, thus no pivot table could be assigned to the variable. If this is the case, the macro notifies the user via a message box and then exits the procedure.

Step 4 of the macro uses a For Each statement to iterate through each pivot field. Each time a new pivot field is selected, you apply all your pivot field restrictions.

How to use the macro

You can implement this kind of a macro in a standard module:

1. **Activate Visual Basic Editor by pressing Alt+F11.**
2. **Right-click the project/workbook name in the project window.**
3. **Choose Insert ⇨ Module.**
4. **Type or paste the code.**

Automatically Deleting Pivot Table Drill-Down Sheets

One of the coolest features of a pivot table is that it gives you the ability to double-click a number and drill into the details. The details are output to a new sheet that you can review. In most cases, you don't want to keep these sheets. In fact, they often become a nuisance because you need to take time to delete them.

This behavior is especially a problem when you distribute pivot table reports to users who frequently drill into details. There is no guarantee that they will remember to clean up the drill-down sheets. Although these sheets probably won't cause issues, they can clutter up the workbook.

Implement the technique described in this section, and your workbook will automatically remove these drill-down sheets.

How the macro works

The basic premise of this macro is simple. When the user clicks for details, outputting a drill-down sheet, the macro renames the output sheet so that the first 10 characters are PivotDrill. Then before the workbook closes, the macro finds any sheet that starts with PivotDrill and deletes it.

The implementation does get a bit tricky because you have two pieces of code. One piece goes in the Worksheet_BeforeDoubleClick event, and the other piece goes into the Workbook_BeforeClose event.

```
Private Sub Worksheet_BeforeDoubleClick(ByVal Target As
        Range, Cancel As Boolean)


'Step 1: Declare your variables
    Dim pt As String


'Step 2: Exit if double-click did not occur on a pivot
        table
    On Error Resume Next
    If IsEmpty(Target) And ActiveCell.PivotField.Name <>
        "" Then
    Cancel = True
    Exit Sub
    End If



'Step 3:  Set the PivotTable object
    pt = ActiveSheet.Range(ActiveCell.Address).PivotTable


'Step 4:  If Drilldowns are enabled, drill down
    If ActiveSheet.PivotTables(pt).EnableDrilldown Then
        Selection.ShowDetail = True

        ActiveSheet.Name = _
        Replace(ActiveSheet.Name, "Sheet", "PivotDrill")
    End If

End Sub
```

Step 1 starts by creating the pt Object variable for your pivot table.

Step 2 checks the double-clicked cell. If the cell is not associated with any pivot table, you cancel the double-click event.

If a pivot table is indeed associated with a cell, Step 3 fills the pt variable with the pivot table.

Step 4 checks the EnableDrillDown property. If it is enabled, you trigger the ShowDetail method. This outputs the drill-down details to a new worksheet.

The macro follows the output and uses the Replace function to rename the output sheet so that the first 10 characters are PivotDrill. The Replace function replaces certain text in an expression with other text. In this case, you replace the word *Sheet* with *PivotDrill* by using Replace(ActiveSheet.Name, "Sheet", "PivotDrill").

Sheet1 becomes PivotDrill1; Sheet12 becomes PivotDrill12, and so on.

Next, the macro sets up the Worksheet_BeforeDoubleClick event. As the name suggests, this code runs when the workbook closes.

```
Private Sub Workbook_BeforeClose(Cancel As Boolean)


'Step 5:  Declare your variables
    Dim ws As Worksheet


'Step 6:  Loop through worksheets
    For Each ws In ThisWorkbook.Worksheets


'Step 7:  Delete any sheet that starts with PivotDrill
        If Left(ws.Name, 10) = "PivotDrill" Then
            Application.DisplayAlerts = False
            ws.Delete
            Application.DisplayAlerts = True
        End If
    Next ws

End Sub
```

Step 5 declares the ws Worksheet variable, which holds worksheet objects as you loop through the workbook.

Step 6 starts the looping, telling Excel that you want to evaluate all worksheets in this workbook.

In the last step, you evaluate the name of the sheet that has focus in the loop. If the left 10 characters of that sheet name are PivotDrill, you delete the worksheet. After all the sheets have been evaluated, all drill-down sheets have been cleaned up and the macro ends.

How to use the macro

To implement the first part of the macro, you need to copy and paste it into the Worksheet_BeforeDoubleClick event code window. Placing the macro here allows it to run each time you double-click the sheet:

1. **Activate Visual Basic Editor by pressing Alt+F11.**

2. **In the project window, find your project/workbook name and click the plus sign next to it to see all the sheets.**

3. **Click the sheet in which you want to trigger the code.**

4. **In the Event drop-down list box, select the BeforeDoubleClick event (see Figure 8-3).**

5. **Type or paste the code.**

Figure 8-3:
Enter your
code in the
Worksheet
Before-
DoubleClick
event.

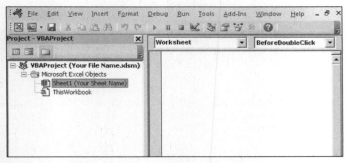

To implement this macro, you need to copy and paste it into the Workbook_ BeforeClose event code window. Placing the macro here allows it to run each time you try to close the workbook:

1. **Activate Visual Basic Editor by pressing Alt+F11.**

2. **In the project window, find your project/workbook name and click the plus sign next to it to see all the sheets.**

3. **Click ThisWorkbook.**

4. **In the Event drop-down list, select the BeforeClose event (see Figure 8-4).**

5. **Type or paste the code.**

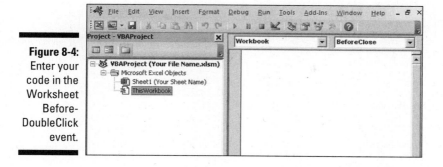

Figure 8-4:
Enter your
code in the
Worksheet
Before-
DoubleClick
event.

Printing a Pivot Table for Each Report Filter Item

Pivot tables provide an excellent mechanism to parse large data sets into printable files. You can build a pivot table report, complete with aggregations and analysis, and then place a field (such as Region) into the report filter. With the report filter, you can select each data item one at a time, and then print the pivot table report.

The macro in this section demonstrates how to automatically iterate through all the values in a report filter and print.

How the macro works

In the Excel object model, the Report Filter drop-down list is known as PageField. To print a pivot table for each data item in a report filter, you need to loop through the PivotItems collection of the PageField object. As you loop, you dynamically change the selection in the report filter, and then use the ActiveSheet.PrintOut method to print the target range.

```
Sub Macro1()

'Step 1: Declare your variables
    Dim pt As PivotTable
    Dim pf As PivotField
    Dim pi As PivotItem
```

```
'Step 2: Point to the pivot table in the active cell
    On Error Resume Next
    Set pt = ActiveSheet.PivotTables(ActiveCell.
        PivotTable.Name)


'Step 3: Exit if active cell is not in a pivot table
    If pt Is Nothing Then
    MsgBox "You must place your cursor inside a pivot
        table."
    Exit Sub
    End If


'Step 4: Exit if more than one page field
    If pt.PageFields.Count > 1 Then
    MsgBox "Too many Report Filter Fields. Limit 1."
    Exit Sub
    End If


'Step 5: Start looping through the page field and its
        pivot items
    For Each pf In pt.PageFields
        For Each pi In pf.PivotItems


'Step 6: Change the selection in the report filter
            pt.PivotFields(pf.Name).CurrentPage = pi.Name


'Step 7: Set print area and print
        ActiveSheet.PageSetup.PrintArea = pt.TableRange2.
            Address
        ActiveSheet.PrintOut Copies:=1


'Step 8: Get the next page field item
        Next pi
    Next pf

End Sub
```

Step 1 declares three variables: pt is the memory container for your pivot table, pf is a memory container for your page fields, and pi holds each pivot item as you loop through the PageField object.

The active cell must be inside a pivot table for this macro to run. The assumption is that when the cursor is inside a particular pivot table, you want to perform the macro action on that pivot.

Step 2 sets the pt variable to the name of the pivot table on which the active cell is found by using the ActiveCell.PivotTable.Name property to get the name of the target pivot.

If the active cell is not inside a pivot table, the macro throws an error. You use the On Error Resume Next statement to tell Excel to continue with the macro if there is an error.

Step 3 checks to see whether the pt variable is filled with a PivotTable object. If the pt variable is set to Nothing, the active cell was not in a pivot table, thus no pivot table could be assigned to the variable. If this is the case, a message box notifies the user and you exit the procedure.

Step 4 determines whether there is more than one report filter field. (If the count of PageFields is greater than 1, there is more than one report filter.) You do this check for a simple reason: You want to avoid printing reports for filters that just happen to be there. Without this check, you might wind up printing hundreds of pages. The macro stops and displays a message box if the field count is greater than 1.

If you need to remove this limitation, simply delete or comment out Step 4 in the macro.

Step 5 starts two loops. The outer loop tells Excel to iterate through all the report filters. The inner loop tells Excel to loop through all the pivot items in the repot filter that currently has focus.

For each pivot item, the macro captures the item name and uses it to change the report filter selection. This effectively alters the pivot table report to match the pivot item.

Step 7 prints the active sheet and then moves to the next pivot item. After you have looped through all pivot items in the report filter, the macro moves to the next PageField. After all PageFields have been evaluated, the macro ends.

How to use the macro

You can implement this kind of a macro in a standard module:

1. **Activate Visual Basic Editor by pressing Alt+F11.**
2. **Right-click the project/workbook name in the project window.**
3. **Choose Insert ⇨ Module.**
4. **Type or paste the code.**

Creating a Workbook for Each Report Filter Item

Pivot tables provide an excellent mechanism to parse large data sets into separate files. You can build a pivot table report, complete with aggregations and analysis, and then place a field (such as Region) into the report filter. With the report filter, you can select each data item one at a time, and then export the pivot table data to a new workbook.

The macro in this section demonstrates how to automatically iterate through all the values in a report filter and export to a new workbook.

How the macro works

In the Excel object model, the Report Filter drop-down list is known as PageField. To print a pivot table for each data item in a report filter, the macro needs to loop through the PivotItems collection of the PageField object. As the macro loops, it must dynamically change the selection in the report filter, and then export the pivot table report to a new workbook.

```
Sub Macro1()

'Step 1: Declare your variables
    Dim pt As PivotTable
    Dim pf As PivotField
    Dim pi As PivotItem


'Step 2: Point to the pivot table in the active cell
    On Error Resume Next
    Set pt = ActiveSheet.PivotTables(ActiveCell.
        PivotTable.Name)


'Step 3:  Exit if active cell is not in a pivot table
    If pt Is Nothing Then
    MsgBox "You must place your cursor inside a pivot
        table."
    Exit Sub
    End If
```

```
'Step 4:  Exit if more than one page field
    If pt.PageFields.Count > 1 Then
    MsgBox "Too many Report Filter Fields. Limit 1."
    Exit Sub
    End If


'Step 5:  Start looping through the page field and its
           pivot items
    For Each pf In pt.PageFields
        For Each pi In pf.PivotItems


'Step 6:  Change the selection in the report filter
           pt.PivotFields(pf.Name).CurrentPage = pi.Name


'Step 7: Copy the data area to a new workbook
           pt.TableRange1.Copy

           Workbooks.Add.Worksheets(1).Paste
           Application.DisplayAlerts = False

           ActiveWorkbook.SaveAs _
           Filename:="C:\Temp\" & pi.Name & ".xlsx"
           ActiveWorkbook.Close
           Application.DisplayAlerts = True


'Step 8: Get the next page field item
        Next pi
    Next pf

End Sub
```

Step 1 declares three variables: pt is the memory container for your pivot table, pf is a memory container for your page fields, and pi holds each pivot item as the macro loops through the PageField object.

The active cell must be inside a pivot table for this macro to run. The assumption is that when the cursor is inside a particular pivot table, you will want to perform the macro action on that pivot.

Step 2 sets the pt variable to name of the pivot table on which the active cell is found. The macro does this by using the ActiveCell.PivotTable.Name property to get the name of the target pivot.

If the active cell is not inside a pivot table, an error is thrown. You use the On Error Resume Next statement to tell Excel to continue with the macro if there is an error.

Step 3 checks to see whether the pt variable is filled with a PivotTable object. If the pt variable is set to Nothing, the active cell was not in a pivot table, thus no pivot table could be assigned to the variable. If this is the case, the macro uses a message box to notify the user and then exits the procedure.

Step 4 determines whether there is more than one report filter field. If the count of PageFields is greater than 1, there is more than one report filter. You do this check to avoid printing reports for filters that just happen to be there. Without this check, you might wind up printing hundreds of pages. The macro stops and displays a message box if the field count is greater than 1.

To remove the one report filter limitation, delete or comment out Step 4 in the macro.

Step 5 starts two loops. The outer loop tells Excel to iterate through all the report filters. The inner loop tells Excel to loop through all the pivot items in the repot filter that currently has focus.

For each pivot item, Step 6 captures the item name and uses it to change the report filter selection. This step effectively alters the pivot table report to match the pivot item.

Step 7 copies TableRange1 of the PivotTable object. TableRange1 is a built-in range object that points to the range of the main data area for the pivot table. You then paste to the data to a new workbook and save it. Note that you need to change the save path to one that works in your environment.

Step 8 moves to the next pivot item. After the macro has looped through all pivot items in the report filter, the macro moves to the next PageField. After all PageFields have been evaluated, the macro ends.

How to use the macro

You can implement this kind of a macro in a standard module:

1. **Activate Visual Basic Editor by pressing Alt+F11.**
2. **Right-click the project/workbook name in the project window.**
3. **Choose Insert ⇨ Module.**
4. **Type or paste the code.**

Resizing All Charts on a Worksheet

When building a dashboard, you often want to achieve symmetry and balance. In many cases, achieving symmetry in your dashboard requires chart size standardization. The macro in this section gives you an easy way to set a standard height and width for all your charts at once.

How the macro works

All charts belong to the ChartObjects collection. To take an action on all charts at one time, you simply iterate through all the charts in ChartObjects. Each chart in the ChartObjects collection has an index number that you can use to bring it into focus. For example, ChartObjects(1) points to the first chart in the sheet.

In this macro, you use this concept to loop through the charts on the active sheet with a simple counter. Each time a new chart is brought into focus, you change its height and width to the size you've defined.

```
Sub Macro1()

'Step 1: Declare your variables
    Dim i As Integer


'Step 2:  Start looping through all the charts
    For i = 1 To ActiveSheet.ChartObjects.Count


'Step 3: Activate each chart and size
    With ActiveSheet.ChartObjects(i)
    .Width = 300
    .Height = 200
    End With



'Step 4:  Increment to move to next chart
    Next i

End Sub
```

Step 1 declares an integer object, variable i, to be used as a looping mechanism.

Step 2 starts the looping by setting i to count from 1 to the maximum number of charts in the ChartObjects collection on the active sheet. When the code starts, i initiates with the number 1. As you loop, the variable increments by 1 sheet.

Step 3 passes i to the ChartObjects collection as the index number to bring a chart into focus. Then the width and height of the chart is set to the number you specify in the code. You can change these numbers to suit your needs.

In Step 4, the macro loops back around to increment i by 1 and get the next chart. After all charts have been evaluated, the macro ends.

How to use the macro

To implement this macro, you can copy and paste it into a standard module:

1. **Activate Visual Basic Editor by pressing Alt+F11.**
2. **Right-click the project/workbook name in the project window.**
3. **Choose Insert ➪ Module.**
4. **Type or paste the code in to the newly created blank module.**

Aligning a Chart to a Specific Range

Along with adjusting the size of charts, many of us spend a good bit of time positioning them so that they align nicely in our dashboards. This macro easily snaps your charts to defined ranges, with perfect positioning every time.

How the macro works

Every chart has four properties that dictate its size and position: Width, Height, Top, and Left. Interestingly enough, every Range object has these same properties. So if you set a chart's Width, Height, Top, and Left properties to match that of a particular range, the chart essentially snaps to that range.

After you decide how you want your dashboard to be laid out, note the ranges that encompass each area of your dashboard. Then use those ranges in this macro to snap each chart to the appropriate range. In this example, you adjust four charts to so that their Width, Height, Top, and Left properties match a given range.

Note that you're identifying each chart with a name. Charts are, by default, named *Chart* and the number in which they were added (Chart 1, Chart 2, Chart 3, and so on). You can see what each chart is named by clicking it, and then going up to the Ribbon and choosing Format ➪ Selection Pane. This command activates a task pane listing all the objects on your sheet, as shown in Figure 8-5.

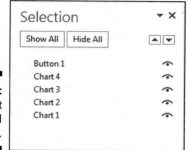

Figure 8-5:
Your chart
objects and
their names.

You can use the Selection task pane to get the appropriate chart names for
your version of this macro.

```
Sub Macro1()

Dim SnapRange As Range

Set SnapRange = ActiveSheet.Range("B6:G19")
    With ActiveSheet.ChartObjects("Chart 1")
     .Height = SnapRange.Height
     .Width = SnapRange.Width
     .Top = SnapRange.Top
     .Left = SnapRange.Left
    End With


Set SnapRange = ActiveSheet.Range("B21:G34")
    With ActiveSheet.ChartObjects("Chart 2")
     .Height = SnapRange.Height
     .Width = SnapRange.Width
     .Top = SnapRange.Top
     .Left = SnapRange.Left
    End With


Set SnapRange = ActiveSheet.Range("I6:Q19")
    With ActiveSheet.ChartObjects("Chart 3")
     .Height = SnapRange.Height
     .Width = SnapRange.Width
     .Top = SnapRange.Top
     .Left = SnapRange.Left
    End With
```

```
Set SnapRange = ActiveSheet.Range("I21:Q34")
    With ActiveSheet.ChartObjects("Chart 4")
    .Height = SnapRange.Height
    .Width = SnapRange.Width
    .Top = SnapRange.Top
    .Left = SnapRange.Left
    End With

End Sub
```

How to use the macro

To implement this macro, you can copy and paste it into a standard module:

1. **Activate Visual Basic Editor by pressing Alt+F11.**
2. **Right-click project/workbook name in the project window.**
3. **Choose Insert ⇨ Module.**
4. **Type or paste the code in to the newly created module.**

Creating a Set of Disconnected Charts

When you need to copy charts from a workbook and paste them elsewhere (in another workbook, in PowerPoint, in Outlook, and so on), it's often best to disconnect them from the original source data. In this way, you won't get any annoying missing link messages that Excel throws. The macro in this section copies all the charts in the active sheet, pastes them into a new workbook, and disconnects them from the original source data.

How the macro works

This macro uses the ShapeRange.Group method to group all the charts on the active sheet into one shape. This action is similar to what you would do if you were to group a set of shapes manually. After the charts are grouped, you copy the group and paste it to a new workbook. You then use the BreakLink method to remove references to the original source data. The BreakLink method ensures that Excel hard-codes the chart data into array formulas.

```
Sub Macro1()

'Step 1:  Declare your variables
Dim wbLinks As Variant


'Step 2:  Group the charts, copy the group, and then
          ungroup
    With ActiveSheet.ChartObjects.ShapeRange.Group
    .Copy
    .Ungroup
    End With


'Step 3:  Paste into a new workbook and ungroup
    Workbooks.Add.Sheets(1).Paste
    Selection.ShapeRange.Ungroup


'Step 4: Break the links
    wbLinks = ActiveWorkbook.LinkSources(Type:=xlLinkType
          ExcelLinks)
    ActiveWorkbook.BreakLink Name:=wbLinks(1), _
                        Type:=xlLinkTypeExcelLinks

End Sub
```

Step 1 declares the wbLinks Variant variable. The macro uses this variable in Step 4 to pass the link source when breaking the links.

Step 2 uses ChartObjects.ShapeRange.Group to group all the charts into a single shape. The macro then copies the group to the clipboard. After the group is copied, the macro ungroups the charts.

Step 3 creates a new workbook and pastes the copied group to Sheet 1. After the group has been pasted, you can ungroup so that each chart is separate again. Note that the newly created workbook is now the active object, so all references to ActiveWorkbook point back to this workbook.

Step 4 captures the link source in the wbLinks variable. The macro then tells Excel to break the links.

This technique converts the chart source links to an array formula, so it can fail if your chart contains too many data points. How many is too many? The number can be different depending on the memory limits of the PC you're working with.

How to use the macro

To implement this macro, you can copy and paste it into a standard module:

1. **Activate Visual Basic Editor by pressing Alt+F11.**
2. **Right-click project/workbook name in the project window.**
3. **Choose Insert ⇨ Module.**
4. **Type or paste the code into the newly created module.**

Printing All Charts on a Worksheet

To manually print a chart, you can click any embedded chart in your work-sheet and then click Print. This action prints the chart on its own sheet without any other data on the sheet. Although manually printing a chart sounds easy enough, but it can become a chore if you have to do it for many charts. This macro makes short work of this task.

How the macro works

All charts belong to the ChartObjects collection. To take an action on all charts at one time, you simply iterate through all the charts in ChartObjects. Each chart in the ChartObjects collection has an index number that you can use to bring it into focus. For example, ChartObjects(1) points to the first chart in the sheet.

In this macro, you use this concept to loop through the charts on the active sheet with a simple counter. Each time a new chart is brought into focus, you print it.

```
Sub Macro1()

'Step 1: Declare your variables
    Dim ChartList As Integer
    Dim i As Integer


'Step 2:  Start looping through all the charts
    For i = 1 To ActiveSheet.ChartObjects.Count
```

```
'Step 3: Activate each chart and print
        ActiveSheet.ChartObjects(i).Activate
        ActiveChart.PageSetup.Orientation = xlLandscape
        ActiveChart.PrintOut Copies:=1


'Step 4:  Increment to move to next chart
    Next i

End Sub
```

Step 1 declares an integer object, variable i, as a looping mechanism.

Step 2 starts the looping by setting i to count from 1 to the maximum number of charts in the ChartObjects collection on the active sheet. When the code starts, i initiates with the number 1. As you loop, the variable increments by 1 until it reaches a number equal to the maximum number of charts on the sheet.

Step 3 passes i to the ChartObjects collection as the index number. This brings a chart into focus. You then use the ActiveChart.Printout method to trigger the print. Note that you can adjust the Orientation property to either xlLandscape or xlPortrait, depending on what you need.

Step 4 loops back around to increment i by one and get the next chart. After all charts have been printed, the macro ends.

How to use the macro

To implement this macro, you can copy and paste it into a standard module:

1. **Activate Visual Basic Editor by pressing Alt+F11.**

2. **Right-click the project/workbook name in the project window.**

3. **Choose Insert ⇨ Module.**

4. **Type or paste the code into the newly created module.**

Chapter 9

Sending Emails from Excel

Did you know that you probably integrate Excel and Outlook all the time? It's true. If you've sent or received an Excel workbook through Outlook, you've integrated the two programs; albeit manually. In this chapter, I show you a few examples of how you can integrate Excel and Outlook in a more automated fashion.

The macros in this chapter automate Microsoft Outlook. For these macros to work, Microsoft Outlook must be installed on your system.

Mailing the Active Workbook as an Attachment

The most fundamental Outlook task you can perform through automation is sending an email. In the sample code in this section, the active workbook is sent to two email recipients as an attachment.

You may noticed that I am not using the SendMail command native to Excel, which enables you to send simple email messages directly from Excel. However, the SendMail command is not as robust as Outlook automation. SendMail does not allow you to attach files or to use the CC and BCC fields in the email. These limitations make the technique used by this section's macro a superior method.

How the macro works

Because this code will be run from Excel, you need to set a reference to Microsoft Outlook Object Library. Open Visual Basic Editor in Excel and choose Tools ⇨ References. Scroll down until you find the entry Microsoft Outlook *xx* Object Library, where the *xx* is your version of Outlook. Select the check box next to the entry.

```
Sub Macro1()

'Step 1:  Declare your variables
    Dim OLApp As Outlook.Application
    Dim OLMail As Object


'Step 2:  Open Outlook and start a new mail item
    Set OLApp = New Outlook.Application
    Set OLMail = OLApp.CreateItem(0)
    OLApp.Session.Logon


'Step 3:  Build your mail item and send
    With OLMail
    .To = "admin@datapigtechnologies.com;
          mike@datapigtechnologies.com"
    .CC = ""
    .BCC = ""
    .Subject = "This is the Subject line"
    .Body = "Sample File Attached"
    .Attachments.Add ActiveWorkbook.FullName
    .Display
    End With


'Step 4:  Memory cleanup
    Set OLMail = Nothing
    Set OLApp = Nothing

End Sub
```

Step 1 declares two variables. OLApp is an Object variable that exposes the Outlook Application object, and OLMail is an Object variable that holds a mail item.

Step 2 activates Outlook and starts a new session. Note that you use OLApp. Session.Logon to log in to the current MAPI session with default credentials. Step 2 also creates a mail item, similar to manually selecting the New Message button in Outlook.

Step 3 builds the profile of your mail item, including the To recipients, CC recipients, BCC recipients, subject, body, and attachments. Note that the recipients are entered in quotes and separates recipients with a semicolon. The standard syntax for an attachment is .Attachments.Add "File Path". In this code, you specify the current workbook's file path with the syntax ActiveWorkbook.Fullname, effectively setting the current workbook as the attachment for the email. When the message has been built, you use the .Display method to review the email. You can replace .Display with .Send to automatically fire off the email without reviewing.

Releasing the objects assigned to your variables is generally good practice to reduce the chance of any problems caused by rouge objects that may remain open in memory. As you can see in Step 4, you simply set the variable to Nothing.

How to use the macro

To implement this macro, you can copy and paste it into a standard module:

1. **Activate Visual Basic Editor by pressing Alt+F11.**

2. **Right-click the project/workbook name in the project window.**

3. **Choose Insert ⇨ Module.**

4. **Type or paste the code into the newly created module.**

Mailing a Specific Range as an Attachment

You may not always want to send your entire workbook through email. The macro in this section demonstrates how to send a specific range of data rather than the entire workbook.

How the macro works

Because this code is run from Excel, you need to set a reference to Microsoft Outlook Object Library. Open Visual Basic Editor in Excel and choose Tools⇨References. Scroll down to the Microsoft Outlook *xx* Object Library entry, where the *xx* is your version of Outlook. Select the check box next to the entry.

```
Sub Macro1()

'Step 1:  Declare your variables
    Dim OLApp As Outlook.Application
    Dim OLMail As Object


'Step 2:  Copy range, paste to new workbook, and save it
    Sheets("Revenue Table").Range("A1:E7").Copy
    Workbooks.Add
    Range("A1").PasteSpecial xlPasteValues
    Range("A1").PasteSpecial xlPasteFormats
    ActiveWorkbook.SaveAs ThisWorkbook.Path & _
            "\TempRangeForEmail.xlsx"


'Step 3:  Open Outlook and start a new mail item
    Set OLApp = New Outlook.Application
    Set OLMail = OLApp.CreateItem(0)
    OLApp.Session.Logon


'Step 4:  Build your mail item and send
    With OLMail
    .To = "admin@datapigtechnologies.com; _
            mike@datapigtechnologies.com"
    .CC = ""
    .BCC = ""
    .Subject = "This is the Subject line"
    .Body = "Sample File Attached"
    .Attachments.Add (ThisWorkbook.Path & _
            "\TempRangeForEmail.xlsx")
    .Display
    End With


'Step 5:  Delete the temporary Excel file
    ActiveWorkbook.Close SaveChanges:=True
    Kill ThisWorkbook.Path & "\TempRangeForEmail.xlsx"


'Step 6:  Memory cleanup
    Set OLMail = Nothing
    Set OLApp = Nothing

End Sub
```

Step 1 declares two variables. OLApp is an Object variable that exposes the Outlook Application object, and OLMail is an Object variable that holds a mail item.

Step 2 copies a specified range and pastes the values and formats to a temporary Excel file. The macro then saves the temporary file, giving it a file path and filename.

Step 3 activates Outlook and starts a new session. Note that you use OLApp. Session.Logon to log in to the current MAPI session with default credentials Step 3 also creates a mail item, similar to manually selecting the New Message button in Outlook.

Step 4 builds the profile of the mail item, including the To recipients, CC recipients, BCC recipients, subject, body, and attachments. Note that the recipients are entered with quotes and separated with a semicolon.

You specify your newly created temporary Excel file path as the attachment for the email. When the message has been built, you use the .Display method to review the email. You can replace .Display with .Send to automatically fire off the email without reviewing it.

You don't want to leave temporary files hanging out there, so after the email has been sent, Step 5 deletes the temporary Excel file you created.

It is generally good practice to release the objects assigned to your variables to reduce the chance of any problems caused by rouge objects that may remain open in memory. In Step 6, you simply set the variable to Nothing.

How to use the macro

To implement this macro, you can copy and paste it into a standard module:

1. **Activate Visual Basic Editor by pressing Alt+F11.**
2. **Right-click the project/workbook name in the project window.**
3. **Choose Insert ⇨ Module.**
4. **Type or paste the code into the newly created module.**

Mailing a Single Sheet as an Attachment

The macro in this section demonstrates how you would send a specific worksheet of data rather than the entire workbook.

How the macro works

Because this code is run from Excel, you need to set a reference to Microsoft Outlook Object Library. Open Visual Basic Editor in Excel and choose Tools ⇨ References. Scroll down to the Microsoft Outlook *xx* Object Library entry, where the *xx* is your version of Outlook. Select the check box next to the entry.

```
Sub Macro1()

'Step 1:  Declare your variables
    Dim OLApp As Outlook.Application
    Dim OLMail As Object


'Step 2:  Copy worksheet, paste to new workbook, and save
          it
    Sheets("Revenue Table").Copy
    ActiveWorkbook.SaveAs ThisWorkbook.Path & _
          "\TempRangeForEmail.xlsx"


'Step 3:  Open Outlook and start a new mail item
    Set OLApp = New Outlook.Application
    Set OLMail = OLApp.CreateItem(0)
    OLApp.Session.Logon


'Step 4:  Build your mail item and send
    With OLMail
    .To = "admin@datapigtechnologies.com;
          mike@datapigtechnologies.com"
    .CC = ""
    .BCC = ""
    .Subject = "This is the Subject line"
    .Body = "Sample File Attached"
    .Attachments.Add (ThisWorkbook.Path & _
          "\TempRangeForEmail.xlsx")
    .Display
    End With


'Step 5:  Delete the temporary Excel file
    ActiveWorkbook.Close SaveChanges:=True
    Kill ThisWorkbook.Path & "\TempRangeForEmail.xlsx"


'Step 6:  Memory cleanup
    Set OLMail = Nothing
    Set OLApp = Nothing

End Sub
```

Step 1 first declares two variables. OLApp is an Object variable that exposes the Outlook Application object, and OLMail is an Object variable that holds a mail item.

Step 2 copies a specified worksheet and pastes the values and formats to a temporary Excel file. You then save the temporary file, giving it a file path and filename.

Step 3 activates Outlook and starts a new session. Note that you use OLApp. Session.Logon to log in to the current MAPI session with default credentials. You also create a mail item. Step 3 also creates a mail item, similar to manually selecting the New Message button in Outlook.

Step 4 builds the profile of the mail item, including the To recipients, CC recipients, BCC recipients, subject, body, and attachments. The recipients are entered in quotes and separated by a semicolon.

In this code, you specify your newly created temporary Excel file path as the attachment for the email. When the message has been built, you use the .Display method to review the email. You can replace .Display with .Send to automatically fire off the email without reviewing it.

You don't want to leave temporary files hanging out there, so after the email has been sent, you delete the temporary Excel file you created.

It is generally good practice to release the objects assigned to your variables to reduce the chance of any problems caused by rouge objects that may remain open in memory. As you can see in the code, you simply set the variable to Nothing.

How to use the macro

To implement this macro, you can copy and paste it into a standard module:

1. **Activate Visual Basic Editor by pressing Alt+F11.**
2. **Right-click the project/workbook name in the project window.**
3. **Choose Insert ⇨ Module.**
4. **Type or paste the code into the newly created module.**

Sending Mail with a Link to Your Workbook

Sometimes, you don't need to send an attachment. Instead, you simply want to send an automated email with a link to a file. The macro in this section does just that.

Note that your users or customers will have to have at least read access to the network or location that is tied to the link.

How the macro works

Because this code is run from Excel, you need to set a reference to Microsoft Outlook Object Library. Open Visual Basic Editor in Excel and choose Tools⇔References. Scroll down to the Microsoft Outlook *xx* Object Library entry, where the *xx* is your version of Outlook. Select the check box next to the entry.

```
Sub Macro1()

'Step 1:  Declare your variables
    Dim OLApp As Outlook.Application
    Dim OLMail As Object


'Step 2:  Open Outlook and start a new mail item
    Set OLApp = New Outlook.Application
    Set OLMail = OLApp.CreateItem(0)
    OLApp.Session.Logon


'Step 3:  Build your mail item and send
    With OLMail
    .To = "admin@datapigtechnologies.com;
          mike@datapigtechnologies.com"
    .CC = ""
    .BCC = ""
    .Subject = "Monthly Report Email with Link"
    .HTMLBody = _
    "<p>Monthly report is ready.  Click to Link to get
          it.</p>" &
    "<p><a SPihref=" & Chr(34) &
          "Z:\Downloads\MonthlyReport.xlsx" & _
    Chr(34) & ">Download Now</a></p>"
```

```
      .Display
      End With


'Step 4:   Memory cleanup
     Set OLMail = Nothing
     Set OLApp = Nothing

End Sub
```

Step 1 declares two variables. OLApp is an Object variable that exposes the Outlook Application object, and OLMail is an Object variable that holds a mail item.

Step 2 activates Outlook and starts a new session. Note that you use OLApp. Session.Logon to log in to the current MAPI session with default credentials. This step also creates a mail item. Step 2 also creates a mail item, similar to manually selecting the New Message button in Outlook.

Step 3 builds the profile of your mail item, including the To recipients, CC recipients, BCC recipients, subject, and HTMLBody.

To create the hyperlink, you need to use the HTMLBody property to pass HTML tags. You can replace the file path address shown in the macro with the address for your file. Note that this macro uses the .Display method, which opens the email for your review. You can replace .Display with .Send to automatically fire off the email without reviewing it.

It is generally good practice to release the objects assigned to your variables to reduce the chance of any problems caused by rouge objects that may remain open in memory. In Step 4, you simply set the variable to Nothing.

How to use the macro

To implement this macro, you can copy and paste it into a standard module:

1. **Activate Visual Basic Editor by pressing Alt+F11.**

2. **Right-click the project/workbook name in the project window.**

3. **Choose Insert ⇨ Module.**

4. **Type or paste the code into the newly created module.**

Mailing All Email Addresses in Your Contact List

Ever need to send out a mass mailing such as a newsletter or a memo? Instead of manually entering each contact's email address, you can run the following macro. In this procedure, you send one email, automatically adding all the email addresses in your contact list to the email.

How the macro works

Because this code is run from Excel, you need to set a reference to Microsoft Outlook Object Library. Open Visual Basic Editor in Excel and choose Tools ⇨ References. Scroll down to the Microsoft Outlook *xx* Object Library entry, where the *xx* is your version of Outlook. Select the check box next to the entry.

```
Sub Macro1()

'Step 1:  Declare your variables
    Dim OLApp As Outlook.Application
    Dim OLMail As Object
    Dim MyCell As Range
    Dim MyContacts As Range


'Step 2:  Define the range to loop through
    Set MyContacts = Sheets("Contact List").
        Range("H2:H21")


'Step 3:  Open Outlook
    Set OLApp = New Outlook.Application
    Set OLMail = OLApp.CreateItem(0)
    OLApp.Session.Logon


'Step 4:  Add each address in the contact list
    With OLMail

            For Each MyCell In MyContacts
            .BCC = .BCC & Chr(59) & MyCell.Value
            Next MyCell

        .Subject = "Sample File Attached"
        .Body = "Sample file is attached"
```

```
            .Attachments.Add ActiveWorkbook.FullName
            .Display

    End With


'Step 5:  Memory cleanup
    Set OLMail = Nothing
    Set OLApp = Nothing

End Sub
```

Step 1 declares four Object variables: OLApp exposes the Outlook Application object, OLMail holds a mail item, MyCell holds an Excel range, and MyContacts holds an Excel range.

Step 2 points the MyContacts variable to the range of cells that contain your email addresses. You'll be looping through this range of cells to add email addresses to your email.

Step 3 activates Outlook and starts a new session. Note that you use OLApp. Session.Logon to log in to the current MAPI session with default credentials. You also create a mail item. Step 3 also creates a mail item, similar to manually selecting the New Message button in Outlook.

Step 4 builds the profile of your mail item. Note that you are looping through each cell in the MyContacts range and adding the contents (which are email addresses) to BCC. You use the BCC property instead of To or CC so that each recipient gets an email that looks as though it was sent only to him or her. Your recipients won't be able to see the other email addresses because they are sent with BCC (Blind Courtesy Copy).

This macro uses the .Display method, which opens the email for your review. You can replace .Display with .Send to automatically fire off the email without reviewing.

It is generally good practice to release the objects assigned to your variables to reduce the chance of any problems caused by rouge objects that may remain open in memory. In Step 5, you simply set the variable to Nothing.

How to use the macro

To implement this macro, you can copy and paste it into a standard module:

1. **Activate Visual Basic Editor by pressing Alt+F11.**
2. **Right-click project/workbook name in the project window.**

3. **Choose Insert ⇨ Module.**

4. **Type or paste the code into the newly created module.**

Saving All Attachments to a Folder

You may often find that certain processes lend themselves to the exchange of data by email. For example, you may send a budget template out for each branch manager to fill out and send back to you by email. Well, if there are 150 branch members, it could be a bit of a pain to save all those email attachments.

The following macro demonstrates one solution to this problem. In this procedure, you use automation to search for all attachments in the inbox and save them to a specified folder.

How the macro works

Because this code is run from Excel, you need to set a reference to Microsoft Outlook Object Library. Open Visual Basic Editor in Excel and choose Tools⇨References. Scroll down to the Microsoft Outlook *xx* Object Library entry, where the *xx* is your version of Outlook. Select the check box next to the entry.

```
Sub Macro1()

'Step 1:  Declare your variables
    Dim ns As Namespace
    Dim MyInbox As MAPIFolder
    Dim MItem As MailItem
    Dim Atmt As Attachment
    Dim FileName As String


'Step 2:  Set a reference to your inbox
    Set ns = GetNamespace("MAPI")
    Set MyInbox = ns.GetDefaultFolder(olFolderInbox)


'Step 3:  Check for messages in your inbox; exit if none
    If MyInbox.Items.Count = 0 Then
    MsgBox "No messages in folder."
    Exit Sub
    End If
```

```
'Step 4:   Create directory to hold attachments
    On Error Resume Next
    MkDir "C:\Temp\MyAttachments\"


'Step 5:   Start to loop through each mail item
    For Each MItem In MyInbox.Items


'Step 6:   Save each attachment and then go to the next
           attachment
    For Each Atmt In MItem.Attachments
    FileName = "C:\Temp\MyAttachments\" & Atmt.FileName
    Atmt.SaveAsFile FileName
    Next Atmt


'Step 7:   Move to the next mail item
    Next MItem


'Step 8:   Memory cleanup
    Set ns = Nothing
    Set MyInbox = Nothing

End Sub
```

Step 1 declares five variables. ns is an object that exposes the MAPI namespace. MyInbox exposes the target mail folder. MItem exposes the properties of a mail item. Atmt is an Object variable that holds an Attachment object. FileName is a String variable that holds the name of the attachment.

Step 2 sets the MyInbox variable to point to the inbox for the default mail client.

Step 3 performs a quick check to make sure that the inbox contains messages. If there are no messages, the macro exits the procedure and displays a message box stating that there are no messages.

Step 4 creates a directory to hold the attachments you find. Although you could use an existing directory, creating a directory specifically for the attachments you save is usually best. Here, you create that directory on the fly. You use On Error Resume Next to ensure that the code does not error out if the directory you're trying to create already exists.

Step 5 starts the loop through each mail item in the target mail folder.

Step 6 ensures that each mail item you loop through is checked for attachments. As you loop, you save each attachment in the specified directory you created.

Step 7 loops back to Step 5 until there are no more mail items to go through.

Releasing the objects assigned to your variables is good general practice because it reduces the chance of any problems caused by rogue objects that may remain open in memory. Step 8 simply sets the variable to Nothing.

How to use it

To implement this macro, you can copy and paste it into a standard module:

1. **Activate Visual Basic Editor by pressing Alt+F11.**
2. **Right-click the project/workbook name in the project window.**
3. **Choose Insert⇨Module.**
4. **Type or paste the code into the newly created module.**

Saving Certain Attachments to a Folder

In the preceding macro, you used automation to search for all attachments in your inbox and to save them to a specified folder. However, in most situations, you probably want to save only certain attachments, such as attachments attached to emails that contain a certain subject. In this example, you get a demonstration of how to check for certain syntax and selectively save attachments.

How the macro works

Because this code is run from Excel, you need to set a reference to Microsoft Outlook Object Library. Open Visual Basic Editor in Excel and choose Tools⇨References. Scroll down to the Microsoft Outlook *xx* Object Library entry, where the *xx* is your version of Outlook. Select the check box next to the entry.

```
Sub Macro1()

'Step 1:  Declare your variables
    Dim ns As Namespace
    Dim MyInbox As MAPIFolder
    Dim MItem As Object
    Dim Atmt As Attachment
    Dim FileName As String
    Dim i As Integer
```

```
'Step 2:  Set a reference to your inbox
    Set ns = GetNamespace("MAPI")
    Set MyInbox = ns.GetDefaultFolder(olFolderInbox)


'Step 3:  Check for messages in your inbox; exit if none
    If MyInbox.Items.Count = 0 Then
    MsgBox "No messages in folder."
    Exit Sub
    End If


'Step 4:  Create directory to hold attachments
    On Error Resume Next
    MkDir "C:\OffTheGrid\MyAttachments\"


'Step 5:  Start to loop through each mail item
    For Each MItem In MyInbox.Items


'Step 6:  Check for the words Data Submission in Subject
          line
    If InStr(1, MItem.Subject, "Data Submission") < 1 Then
    GoTo SkipIt
    End If


'Step 7:  Save each attachment with a log number
    i = 0
    For Each Atmt In MItem.Attachments
    FileName = _
    "C:\Temp\MyAttachments\Attachment-" & i & "-" &
          Atmt.FileName
    Atmt.SaveAsFile FileName
    i = i + 1
    Next Atmt


'Step 8:  Move to the next mail item
SkipIt:
    Next MItem


'Step 9:  Memory cleanup
    Set ns = Nothing
    Set MyInbox = Nothing

End Sub
```

Step 1 first declares six variables. ns is an object that exposse the MAPI namespace. MyInbox exposes the target mail folder. MItem exposes the properties of a mail item. Atmt is an Object variable that holds an Attachment object. FileName is a String variable that holds the name of the attachment. i is an Integer variable used to ensure that each attachment is saved as a unique name.

Step 2 sets the MyInbox variable to point to the inbox for your default mail client.

Step 3 performs a quick check to make sure that your inbox contains messages. If there are no messages, it exits the procedure and displays a message box stating that there are no messages.

Step 4 creates a directory to hold the attachments you find. Note that it uses On Error Resume Next to ensure that the code does not error out if the directory you're trying to create already exists.

Step 5 starts the loop through each mail item in the target mail folder.

In Step 6, you use the Instr function to check whether the string "Data Submission" is in the subject line of the email. If that string does not exist, you don't care about any attachments to that message. Therefore, you force the code to go to the SkipIt reference (in Step 8). The line of code immediately following the SkipIt reference is essentially a Move Next command, telling the procedure to move to the next mail item.

Step 7 loops through and saves each attachment in the specified directory you created. You add a running integer to the name of each attachment to ensure that each one is saved as a unique name, to avoid overwriting attachments.

Step 8 loops back to Step 5 until there are no more mail items to go through.

Releasing the objects assigned to your variables is generally good practice because it reduces the chance of any problems caused by rouge objects that may remain open in memory. In Step 9, you simply set the variable to Nothing.

How to use the macro

To implement this macro, you can copy and paste it into a standard module:

1. **Activate Visual Basic Editor by pressing Alt+F11.**

2. **Right-click the project/workbook name in the project window.**

3. **Choose Insert ⇨ Module.**

4. **Type or paste the code into the newly created module.**

Part V
The Part of Tens

Discover ten jobs that are available for Excel analysts who have Excel macro skills in the article found at www.dummies.com/extras/excelmacros.

In this part . . .

✔ Take a look at a few tricks that help you more efficiently use Visual Basic Editor.

✔ Discover some of the debugging tips for avoiding errors in your VBA code.

✔ Learn how to most effectively use the Excel Help system when searching for VBA help.

✔ Gain insight into some of the resources available online to further your macro skills.

Chapter 10

Ten Handy Visual Basic Editor Tips

*I*f you're going to be spending time working with macros in Visual Basic Editor, why not take advantage of a few of the built-in tools that will make your job easier? Whether you're a fresh-faced analyst new to programming, or a jaded veteran living on Mountain Dew and sunflower seeds, these tips will greatly improve your macro programming experience.

Applying Block Comments

Placing a single apostrophe in front of any line of code tells Excel to skip that line of code. This technique is called commenting out code. Most programmers use the single apostrophe to create comments or notes in the code, as shown in Figure 10-1.

It's sometimes beneficial to comment out multiple lines of code. This way, you can test certain lines of code while telling Excel to ignore the commented lines.

```
'Declare your Variables
    Dim ws As Worksheet

'Avoid Error if no formulas are found
    On Error Resume Next

'Start looping through worksheets
    For Each ws In ActiveWorkbook.Worksheets

'Select cells and highlight them
    With ws.Cells.SpecialCells(xlCellTypeFormulas)
    .Interior.ColorIndex = 36
    End With

'Get next worksheet
    Next ws
```

Figure 10-1:
A single
apostrophe
in front of
any line
turns that
line into a
comment.

Instead of spending time commenting out one line at a time, you can use the Edit toolbar to comment out an entire block of code.

To activate the Edit toolbar, go to the VBE menu and choose View⇨ Toolbars⇨Edit. Select the lines of code you want commented out and then click the Comment Block icon on the Edit toolbar, as shown in Figure 10-2.

TIP

You can ensure that the Edit toolbar is always visible by dragging it up to the VBE menu. It will anchor itself to the location you choose.

Figure 10-2:
Use the
Edit toolbar
to apply
comments
to a block
of code.

Remove comment

Apply comment

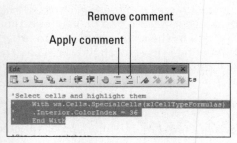

Copying Multiple Lines of Code

You can copy entire blocks of code by highlighting the lines you need, and then holding down the Ctrl key while dragging the block. This old Windows trick works even when you drag across modules.

You'll know that you are dragging a copy when your cursor shows a plus symbol next to it, as shown in Figure 10-3.

```
'Define the target Range.
    Set MyRange = ActiveSheet.UsedRange

'Start reverse looping through the range.
    For iCounter = MyRange.Columns.Count To 1 Step -1

'If entire column is empty then delete it.
        If Application.CountA(Columns(iCounter).EntireColumn) = 0 Then
        Columns(iCounter).Delete
        End If
```

Jumping between Modules and Procedures

After your cache of macro code starts to grow, it can be a pain to quickly move between modules and procedures. You can ease the pain by using a few hot keys.

✔ Press **Ctrl+Tab** to quickly move between modules.

✔ Press **Ctrl+Page Up** and **Ctrl+Page Down** to move between procedures within a module.

Teleporting to Your Functions

When reviewing a macro, you may encounter a variable or a function name that is obviously pointing to some other piece of code. Instead of scouring through all modules to find where that function or variable name comes from, you can simply place your cursor on that function or variable name and press Shift+F2.

As Figure 10-4 illustrates, you are instantly teleported to the origin of that function or variable name. Pressing Ctrl+Shift+F2 will take you back to where you started.

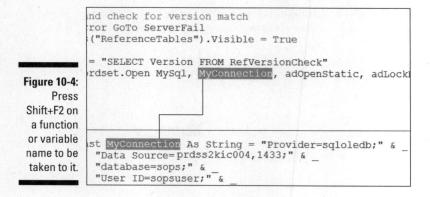

Figure 10-4:
Press
Shift+F2 on
a function
or variable
name to be
taken to it.

Staying in the Right Procedure

When your modules contain multiple procedures, scrolling through a particular procedure without inadvertently scrolling into another procedure can be difficult. You will often find yourself scrolling up and then down, trying to get back to the correct piece of code.

To avoid this nonsense, click the Procedure View button at the lower-left corner of VBE, as shown in Figure 10-5. Doing so limits scrolling to only the procedure you're in.

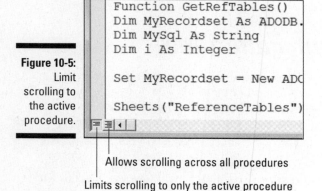

Figure 10-5:
Limit
scrolling to
the active
procedure.

Allows scrolling across all procedures

Limits scrolling to only the active procedure

Stepping through Your Code

VBA offers several tools to help you debug your code. In programming, the term *debugging* means finding and correcting possible errors in code.

One of the more useful debugging tools is the capability to step through your code one line at a time. When you step through code, you are watching each line get executed.

To step through your code, you need to put your macro in debug mode. Simply place your cursor anywhere in your macro and then press the F8 key.

The first line of code is highlighted and a small arrow appears on the code window's left margin, as shown in Figure 10-6. Press F8 again to execute the highlighted line of code and move to the next line. Keep pressing F8 to watch each line get executed until the end of the macro.

```
'Declare your variables.
    Dim MyRange As Range
    Dim iCounter As Long

'Define the target Range.
    Set MyRange = ActiveSheet.UsedRange

'Start reverse looping through the range.
    For iCounter = MyRange.Columns.Count To 1 Step -1
        iCounter = 12
'If entire column is empty then delete it.
        If Application.CountA(Columns(iCounter).EntireColumn) = 0 Then
        Columns(iCounter).Delete
        End If


'Step 5: Increment the counter down
    Next iCounter
```

Figure 10-6:
Press F8 to step through each line of your macro.

As a bonus, while stepping through the code, you can hover over any String or Integer variable to see the current value of that variable.

To get out of debug mode, go up to the VBE menu and choose Debug⇨Step Out.

Stepping to a Specific Code Line

In the last example, you saw how you can step through your code by placing the cursor anywhere in the macro and then pressing F8. Your macro goes into debug mode. The first line of code is highlighted and a small arrow appears in the code window's left margin.

This is great, but what if you want to start stepping through your code at a specific line? Well, you can do just that by simply moving the arrow!

When a line of code is highlighted in debug mode, you can click and drag the arrow in the left margin of the code window upward or downward, dropping it at whichever line of code you want to execute next, as shown in Figure 10-7.

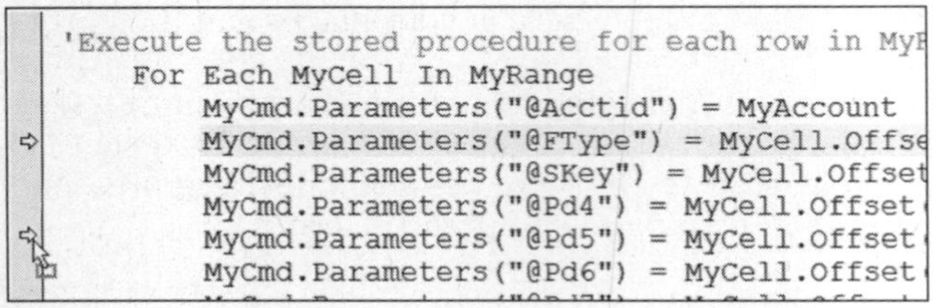

Figure 10-7:
Drag the
arrow while
stepping
through
your code.

```
'Execute the stored procedure for each row in MyR
    For Each MyCell In MyRange
        MyCmd.Parameters("@Acctid") = MyAccount
        MyCmd.Parameters("@FType") = MyCell.Offse
        MyCmd.Parameters("@SKey") = MyCell.Offset
        MyCmd.Parameters("@Pd4") = MyCell.Offset
        MyCmd.Parameters("@Pd5") = MyCell.Offset
        MyCmd.Parameters("@Pd6") = MyCell.Offset
```

Stopping Code at a Predefined Point

Another useful debugging tool is the ability to set a breakpoint in your code. When you set a breakpoint, your code will run as normal and then halt at the line of code where you defined as the breakpoint.

This debugging technique comes in handy when you want to run tests small blocks of code at a time. For example, if you suspect there may be an error in your macro but you know that the majority of the macro runs without any problems, you can set a breakpoint starting at the suspect line of code then run the macro. When the macro reaches your breakpoint, execution halts. At this point, you can then press the F8 key on your keyboard to watch as the macro runs one line at a time.

To set a breakpoint in your code, place your cursor where you want the breakpoint to start, and then press the F9 key on your keyboard. As Figure 10-8 demonstrates, VBA will clearly mark the breakpoint with a dot in the Code window's left margin, and the code line itself will be shaded maroon.

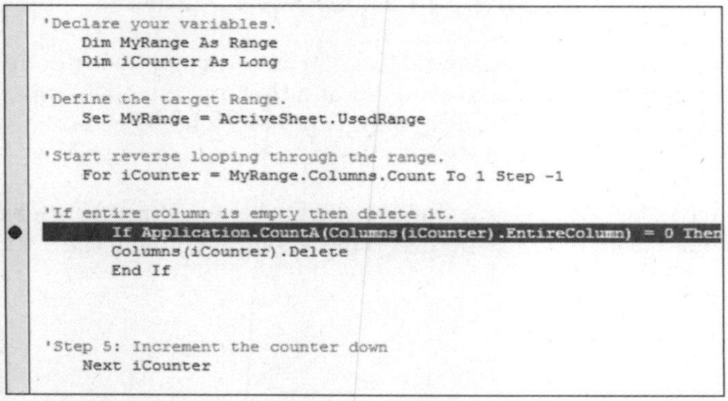

Figure 10-8:
A breakpoint
is marked
by a dot and
shaded text.

```
'Declare your variables.
    Dim MyRange As Range
    Dim iCounter As Long

'Define the target Range.
    Set MyRange = ActiveSheet.UsedRange

'Start reverse looping through the range.
    For iCounter = MyRange.Columns.Count To 1 Step -1

'If entire column is empty then delete it.
        If Application.CountA(Columns(iCounter).EntireColumn) = 0 Then
            Columns(iCounter).Delete
        End If


'Step 5: Increment the counter down
    Next iCounter
```

When your macro hits a breakpoint, it will effectively be placed into debug mode. To get out of debug mode, you can go up to the VBE menu and select Debug⇨Step Out.

Seeing Beginning and Ending Variable Values

If you hover over a String or Integer variable in VBA while in debug mode, you can see the value of that variable in a tooltip. This feature allows you to see the values that are being passed in and out of variables, which is useful when debugging code.

However, tooltips can hold only 77 characters (including the variable name), so if the value in your variable is too long, it gets cut off. To see beyond the first 77 characters, simply hold down the Ctrl key while you hover.

Figure 10-9 demonstrates what the tooltip looks like when hovering over a variable in debug mode.

```
Set XL = CreateObject("Excel.Application")

FileCopy RawDataFile, TempDataFile
    TempDataFile = "C:\Monthly Epi Process\Finance Feeds\Temp Finance Data Raw F...
XL.workbooks.Open TempDataFile

Select Case Month(Date) - 1
```

Hover over variable to see the beginning characters

```
Set XL = CreateObject("Excel.Application")

FileCopy RawDataFile, TempDataFile
    TempDataFile = ...ly Epi Process\Finance Feeds\Temp Finance Data Raw File.xls"
XL.workbooks.Open TempDataFile

Select Case Month(Date) - 1
```

Press the Ctrl key while hovering over variable to see the ending characters

Figure 10-9: The beginning and ending characters in a variable tooltip.

Turning Off Auto Syntax Check

Often times, while working on some code, you'll find that you need to go to another line to copy something. You're not finished with the line; you just need to leave it for a second. But VBE immediately stops you in your tracks with an error message, similar to the one shown in Figure 10-10, warning you about something you already know.

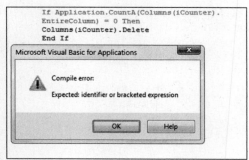

Figure 10-10:
An
unfinished
line of code
results in a
jarring error
message.

These message boxes force you to stop what you're doing to acknowledge the error by pressing the OK button. After a half-day of these abrupt message boxes, you'll be ready to throw your computer against the wall.

Well, you can save your computer and your sanity by turning off Auto Syntax Check. Go up to the VBE menu and choose Tools⇨Options. The Options dialog box appears, displaying the Editor tab shown in Figure 10-11. Deselect the Auto Syntax Check option to stop these annoying error messages.

Don't worry about missing a legitimate mistake. Your code will still turn red if you goof up, providing a visual indication that something is wrong.

Figure 10-11:
Prevent
warning
messages
while
coding.

Chapter 11

Ten Places to Turn for Macro Help

*N*o one can become a macro expert in one day. VBA is a journey of time and practice. The good news is that there are plenty of resources out there that can help you on your path. In this chapter, you'll discover ten of the most useful places to turn to when you need an extra push in the right direction.

Letting Excel Write the Macro for You

One of the best places to get macro help is Macro Recorder in Excel. When you record a macro with Macro Recorder, Excel writes the underlying VBA for you. After recording, you can review the code; see what the recorder is doing, and then try to turn the code it creates into something more suited to your needs.

For example, let's say you need a macro that refreshes all the pivot tables in your workbook and clears all the filters in each pivot table. Writing this macro from a blank canvas would be a daunting task. Instead, you can start Macro Recorder and record yourself refreshing all the pivot tables and clearing all the filters. When you stop recording, review the macro and make any changes you deem necessary.

Using the VBA Help Files

To a new Excel user, the Help system may seem like a clunky add-on that returns a perplexing list of topics that has nothing to do with the original topic being searched. However, if you learn how to use the Excel Help system effectively, it will often be the fastest and easiest way to get help on a topic.

You need to remember two basic tenants of the Excel Help system:

- ✔ **Location matters when asking for help.** Excel has two Help systems. One provides help with Excel features and the other provides help with VBA programming topics. Instead of doing a global search with your criteria, Excel throws your search criteria only against the Help system relevant to your current location, so the help you get is determined by the area of Excel in which you're working. If you need help on a topic that involves macros and VBA programming, for example, you'll need to be in VBA Editor when you perform your search.

- ✔ **Online help is better than offline help.** When you search for help on a topic, Excel checks to see whether you're connected to the Internet. If you are, Excel returns help results based on online content from Microsoft's website. If you aren't, Excel uses the Help files that are stored locally with Microsoft Office. One way to maximize the help you get in Excel is to use the online help. Online help is generally better than offline help because the content you find with online help is often more detailed and includes updated information, as well as links to other resources not available offline.

Pilfering Code from the Internet

The dirty secret about programming in the Internet age is that there is no longer any original code. All the macro syntax that anyone will ever need has been documented somewhere on the Internet. In many ways, programming has become less about the code one creates from scratch and more about how to take existing code and apply it creatively to a particular scenario.

If you're stuck trying to create a macro for a particular task, fire up your favorite online search engine and describe the task you're trying to accomplish. For the best results, enter *Excel VBA* before your description.

For example, if you're trying to write a macro that deletes all blank rows in a worksheet, search for *Excel VBA delete blank rows in a worksheet.* You can bet that someone on the Internet has tackled the same problem, and you'll find example code that will give you the nugget of information you need to jump-start ideas for building your own macro.

Leveraging User Forums

If you find yourself in a bind, you can post your question in a forum and get customized guidance. *User forums* are online communities that revolve around a particular topic. In these forums, you can post a question and experts will offer advice. The folks answering the questions are typically volunteers who have a passion for helping the community solve real-world challenges.

Many forums are dedicated to all things Excel. To find an Excel forum, enter the words *Excel forum* in your favorite online search engine.

Here are a few tips for getting the most out of user forums:

- ✔ **Read and follow the forum rules before you get started.** These rules often include advice on posting question and community etiquette guidelines.

- ✔ **Use a concise and accurate subject title for your question.** Don't create forum questions with vague titles such as *Need advice* or *Please help*.

- ✔ **Keep the scope of your question narrow.** Don't ask questions like, "How do I build an invoicing macro in Excel?"

- ✔ **Be patient.** Remember that the folks answering your question are volunteers who typically have day jobs. Give the community some time to answer your question.

- ✔ **Check back often.** After posting your question, you may receive requests for more details about your scenario. Do everyone a favor and return to your posting to either review the answers or respond to follow-up questions.

- ✔ **Thank the expert who answered your question.** Take a moment to post a thank-you to the expert who helped you out.

Visiting Expert Blogs

Several dedicated Excel gurus share their knowledge through blogs. These blogs are often treasure troves of tips and tricks, offering nuggets that can help build your skills. Best of all, they're free!

Although these blogs will not necessarily speak to your particular needs, they do offer articles that advance your knowledge of Excel and can even provide general guidance on how to apply Excel in practical business situations.

Here is a list of a few of the best Excel blogs on the Internet today:

- ✔ **ExcelGuru:** Ken Puls is a Microsoft Excel MVP who shares knowledge on his blog (`www.excelguru.ca/blog`). In addition to his blog, Ken offers several learning resources for advancing your knowledge in Excel.

- ✔ **Chandoo.org:** Purna "Chandoo" Duggirala is a Microsoft Excel MVP out of India who burst on the scene in 2007. His innovative blog (`http://chandoo.org/`) offers many free templates and article that are aimed at "making you awesome in Excel."

- ✔ **Contextures:** Debra Dalgleish is a Microsoft Excel MVP and the owner of a popular Excel site (`www.contextures.com`). With an alphabetized list of over 350 Excel topics, the site is sure to provide you with something of interest.

- ✔ **DailyDose:** Dick Kusleika is the owner of the longest-running Excel blog (`www.dailydoseofexcel.com`). He is the king of Excel VBA blogging, with over ten years' worth of articles and examples.

- ✔ **MrExcel:** Bill Jelen is a larger-than-life ambassador of Excel. This long-time Excel MVP offers over a thousand free videos and a huge library of training resources on his site (`www.mrexcel.com`).

Mining YouTube for Video Training

Some of us learn better if we watch a task being done. If you find that you absorb video training better than online articles, consider mining YouTube. You might be surprised at how many free high-quality video tutorials you can find, run by amazing folks who have a passion for sharing knowledge.

Go to `www.YouTube.com` and search for the words *Excel VBA*.

Attending Live and Online Training Classes

Live and online training events are an awesome way to absorb Excel knowledge from a diverse group of people. Not only is the instructor feeding you techniques, but the lively discussions during the class can provide a wealth of ideas and new tips. If you thrive in the energy of live training events, consider searching for Excel classes.

Here are a few site that provide excellent instructor-led Excel courses:

- **Excel Hero Academy:** `http://academy.excelhero.com/excel-hero-academy-tuition`
- **Chandoo.org:** `http://chandoo.org/wp/vba-classes`
- **Exceljet:** `https://exceljet.net`

Learning from Microsoft Office Dev Center

The Microsoft Office Dev Center site is dedicated to helping new developers get a quick start in programming Office products. You can get to the Excel portion of this site by going to `https://msdn.microsoft.com/en-us/library/office/fp179694.aspx`.

Although the site can be a bit difficult to navigate, it's worth a visit to see all the free resources, including sample code, tools, and step-by-step instructions.

Dissecting Other Excel Files in Your Organization

Like finding gold in your backyard, the existing files in your organization are often a treasure trove for learning. Open Excel files that contain macros, and see how others in your organization use them. Try to go through the macros line-by-line and see if you can spot new techniques.

You could find a few new tricks you never thought of. You may even stumble upon entire chunks of useful code you can copy and implement in your own workbooks.

Asking Your Local Excel Genius

Do you have an Excel genius in your company, department, organization, or community? Make friends with that person today. You'll have your own personal Excel forum.

Most Excel experts love sharing their knowledge. So don't be afraid to approach your local Excel guru to ask questions or seek out advice on how to tackle certain macro problems.

Chapter 12

Ten Ways to Speed Up Your Macros

As your macros become increasingly robust and complex, you may find that they lose performance. When discussing macros, the word *performance* is usually synonymous with *speed*. Speed is how quickly your VBA procedures perform their intended tasks.

You can take steps to improve the performance of your macros. In this chapter, you find ten ways to help keep your Excel macros running at their optimum performance level.

Halting Sheet Calculations

Did you know that each time a cell that affects any formula in your spreadsheet is changed or manipulated, Excel recalculates the entire worksheet?

In worksheets that have a large amount of formulas, this behavior can drastically slow down your macros.

If your workbook is formula intensive, you may not want Excel to trigger a recalculation every time a cell value is altered by your macro. You can use the Application.Calculation property to tell Excel to switch to manual calculation mode.

When a workbook is in manual calculation mode, the workbook will not recalculate until you explicitly trigger a calculation by pressing the F9 key.

Turning off the automatic calculation behavior of Excel can dramatically speed up your macro. The idea is to place Excel into manual calculation mode, run your code, and then switch back to automatic calculation mode.

```
Sub Macro1()

Application.Calculation = xlCalculationManual

'Place your macro code here

Application.Calculation = xlCalculationAutomatic

End Sub
```

Setting the calculation mode back to xlCalculationAutomatic will automatically trigger a recalculation of the worksheet, so there is no need to press the F9 key after your macro runs.

If your macro relies on updated values during processing, you'll want to force a calculation so that the macro has the latest values. You can force Excel to calculate by using the Application.Calculate method. Simply enter Application.Caculate as a line in your code where appropriate.

Disabling Sheet Screen Updating

You may notice that when your macros run, your screen does a fair amount of flickering. This flickering is Excel trying to redraw the screen to show the current state of the worksheet. Unfortunately, each time Excel redraws the screen, it takes up memory resources. In most cases, you don't need Excel using up resources to redraw the screen each time your macro performs some action.

In addition to setting the calculation mode to manual, you can use the Application.ScreenUpdating property to disable screen updates until your macro has completed. Disabling screen updating saves time and resources, allowing your macro to run a little faster. After your macro code has finished running, you can turn screen updating back on.

```
Sub Macro1()

Application.Calculation = xlCalculationManual
Application.ScreenUpdating = False

'Place your macro code here

Application.Calculation = xlCalculationAutomatic
Application.ScreenUpdating = True

End Sub
```

After you set the ScreenUpdating property back to True, Excel will automatically trigger a redraw of the screen.

Turning Off Status Bar Updates

The Excel status bar, which appears at the bottom of the Excel window, normally displays the progress of certain actions in Excel. For example, if you copy and paste a range, Excel will show the progress of that operation on the status bar. Often times, the action is performed so fast that you don't see the status bar progress. However, if your macro is working with lots of data, the status bar will take up some resources.

It's important to note that turning off screen updating is separate from turning off the status bar display. That is to say, the status bar will continue to be updated even if you disable screen updating. You can use the Application. DisplayStatusBar property to temporarily disable any status bar updates, further improving the performance of your macro:

```
Sub Macro1()

Application.Calculation = xlCalculationManual
Application.ScreenUpdating = False
Application.DisplayStatusBar = False

'Place your macro code here

Application.Calculation = xlCalculationAutomatic
Application.ScreenUpdating = True
Application.DisplayStatusBar = True

End Sub
```

Telling Excel to Ignore Events

As discussed in Chapter 3, you can implement macros as event procedures, telling Excel to run certain code when a worksheet or workbook changes.

Sometimes, standard macros make changes that will trigger an event procedure. For instance, suppose you have a Worksheet_Change event implemented for Sheet1 of your workbook. Any time a cell or a range is altered, the Worksheet_Change event will fire.

So if you have a standard macro that manipulates several cells on Sheet1, each time a cell on that sheet is changed, your macro has to pause while the Worksheet_Change event runs. You can imagine how this behavior would slow down your macro.

You can add another level of performance boosting by using the EnableEvents property to tell Excel to ignore events while your macro runs.

Simply set the EnableEvents property to False before running your macro. After your macro code is finished running, you can set the EnableEvents property back to True.

```
Sub Macro1()

Application.Calculation = xlCalculationManual
Application.ScreenUpdating = False
Application.DisplayStatusBar = False
Application.EnableEvents = False

'Place your macro code here

Application.Calculation = xlCalculationAutomatic
Application.ScreenUpdating = True
Application.DisplayStatusBar = True
Application.EnableEvents = True

End Sub
```

Although disabling events can indeed speed up your macros, you may need some events to trigger while your macro runs. Be sure to think about your specific scenario and determine what will happen if your worksheet or workbook events are turned off while your macro runs.

Hiding Page Breaks

Another opportunity for a performance boost can be found in page breaks. Each time your macro modifies the number of rows, modifies the number of columns, or alters the page setup of a worksheet, Excel is forced to take time recalculating the page breaks shown on the sheet.

You can avoid this behavior by simply hiding the page breaks before starting your macro.

Set the DisplayPageBreaks sheet property to False to hide page breaks. If you want to continue to show page breaks after your macro runs, set the DisplayPageBreaks sheet property back to True.

```
Sub Macro1()

Application.Calculation = xlCalculationManual
Application.ScreenUpdating = False
Application.DisplayStatusBar = False
Application.EnableEvents = False
Activesheet.DisplayPageBreaks = False

'Place your macro code here

Application.Calculation = xlCalculationAutomatic
Application.ScreenUpdating = True
Application.DisplayStatusBar = True
Application.EnableEvents = True
Activesheet.DisplayPageBreaks = True

End Sub
```

Suspending Pivot Table Updates

If your macro manipulates pivot tables that contain large data sources, you may experience poor performance when doing things like dynamically adding or moving pivot fields. Each change you make to the structure of the pivot table requires Excel to recalculate the values in the pivot table for each pivot field your macro touches.

You can improve the performance of your macro by suspending the recalculation of the pivot table until all pivot field changes have been made. Simply set the PivotTable.ManualUpdate property to True to defer recalculation, run your macro code, and then set the PivotTable.ManualUpdate property back to False to trigger the recalculation.

```
Sub Macro1()

ActiveSheet.PivotTables("PivotTable1").ManualUpdate=True

'Place your macro code here

ActiveSheet.PivotTables("PivotTable1").ManualUpdate=False

End Sub
```

Steering Clear of Copy and Paste

It's important to remember that although Macro Recorder saves time by writing VBA code for you, it does not always write the most efficient code. A prime example is how Macro Recorder captures any copy-and-paste action you perform while recording.

If you were to copy cell A1 and paste it into cell B1 while recording a macro, Macro Recorder would capture the following:

```
Range("A1").Select

Selection.Copy

Range("B1").Select

ActiveSheet.Paste
```

Although this code will indeed copy from cell A1 and paste into B1, it forces Excel to utilize the clipboard, which adds a kind of middleman where there does not need to be one.

You can give your macros a slight boost by cutting out the middleman and performing a direct copy from one cell to a destination cell. This alternate code uses the Destination argument to bypass the clipboard and copy the contents of cell A1 directly to cell B1.

```
Range("A1").Copy Destination:=Range("B1")
```

If you need to copy only values (not formatting or formulas), you can improve performance even more by avoiding the Copy method all together. Simply set the value of the destination cell to the same value found in the source cell. This method is about approximately 25 times faster than using the Copy method:

```
Range("B1").Value = Range("A1").Value
```

If you need to copy only formulas from one cell to another (not values or formatting), you can set the formula of the destination cell to the same formula contained in the source cell:

```
Range("B1").Formula = Range("A1").Formula
```

Using the With Statement

When recording macros, you will often manipulate the same object more than once. For example, your code may change the formatting of cell A1 so that it is underlined, italicized, and formatted bold. If you were to record a macro that applies these formatting options to cell A1, you would get something like this:

```
Range("A1").Select
Selection.Font.Bold = True
Selection.Font.Italic = True
Selection.Font.Underline = xlUnderlineStyleSingle
```

Unfortunately, this code is not as efficient as it could be because it forces Excel to select and then change each property separately.

You can save time and improve performance by using the With statement to perform several actions on a given object in one shot.

The With statement utilized in the following example tells Excel to apply all the formatting changes at one time:

```
With Range("A1").Font

.Bold = True
.Italic = True
.Underline = xlUnderlineStyleSingle

End With
```

Getting into the habit of chunking actions into With statements will not only keep your macros running faster but also make it easier to read your macro code.

Avoiding the Select Method

If you were to record a macro while entering the value 1000 in cell A1 for multiple sheets, you would end up with code that looks similar to the following:

```
Sheets("Sheet1").Select
Range("A1").Select
ActiveCell.FormulaR1C1 = "1000"

Sheets("Sheet2").Select
Range("A1").Select
ActiveCell.FormulaR1C1 = "1000"

Sheets("Sheet3").Select
Range("A1").Select
ActiveCell.FormulaR1C1 = "1000"
```

As you can see, Macro Recorder is fond of using the Select method to explicitly select objects before taking actions on them. Although this code will run fine, it is not efficient because it forces Excel to take the time to explicitly select each object that is being manipulated.

There is generally no need to select objects before working with them. In fact, you can dramatically improve macro performance by not using the Select method.

After recording your macros, make it a habit to alter the generated code to remove the Select methods. In this case, the optimized code would look like the following:

```
Sheets("Sheet1").Range("A1").FormulaR1C1 = "1000"
Sheets("Sheet2").Range("A1").FormulaR1C1 = "1000"
Sheets("Sheet3").Range("A1").FormulaR1C1 = "1000"
```

Note that the nothing is being selected. The code simply uses the object hierarchy to apply the needed actions.

Limiting Trips to the Worksheet

Another way to speed up your macros is to limit the amount of times you reference worksheet data in your code. It is always less efficient to grab data from the worksheet than from memory. That is to say, your macros will run much faster if they do not have to repeatedly interact with the worksheet.

For instance, the following simple code forces VBA to continuously return to Sheets("Sheet1").Range("A1") to get the number needed for the comparison being performed in the If statement:

```
For ReportMonth = 1 To 12

     If Range("A1").Value = ReportMonth Then
     MsgBox 1000000 / ReportMonth

End If

Next ReportMonth
```

A much more efficient method is to save the value in Sheets("Sheet1"). Range("A1") to a variable called MyMonth. This way, the code references the MyMonth variable instead of the worksheet:

```
Dim MyMonth as Integer
MyMonth = Range("A1").Value

For ReportMonth = 1 To 12
If MyMonth = ReportMonth Then
MsgBox 1000000 / ReportMonth
End If

Next ReportMonth
```

Consider leveraging variables to work with data in memory as opposed to directly referencing worksheets.

Index

• **Q** •

• R •

• Y •

• Z •

About the Author

Mike Alexander is a Microsoft Certified Application Developer (MCAD) with more than 15 years' experience consulting and developing office solutions. He is the author of over a dozen books on business analysis using Microsoft Excel and Access. He has been named Microsoft Excel MVP for his contributions to the Excel community. Visit Mike at www.DataPigTechnologies.com, where he offers free Excel and Access training.

Dedication

For my family.

Author's Acknowledgments

My deepest thanks to everyone who helped bring this book to fruition. And a special thank you to Mary, who will open this book long enough to read the dedication and acknowledgments.

Publisher's Acknowledgments

Acquisitions Editor: Katie Mohr

Project Editor: Susan Pink

Copy Editor: Susan Pink

Technical Editors: Mike Talley

Editorial Assistant: Claire Brock

Sr. Editorial Assistant: Cherie Case

Project Editor: Suresh Srinivasan

Cover Image: ©Getty Images/Roz Woodward

Apple & Mac

iPad For Dummies,
6th Edition
978-1-118-72306-7

iPhone For Dummies,
7th Edition
978-1-118-69083-3

Macs All-in-One
For Dummies, 4th Edition
978-1-118-82210-4

OS X Mavericks
For Dummies
978-1-118-69188-5

Blogging & Social Media

Facebook For Dummies,
5th Edition
978-1-118-63312-0

Social Media Engagement
For Dummies
978-1-118-53019-1

WordPress For Dummies,
6th Edition
978-1-118-79161-5

Business

Stock Investing
For Dummies, 4th Edition
978-1-118-37678-2

Investing For Dummies,
6th Edition
978-0-470-90545-6

Personal Finance
For Dummies, 7th Edition
978-1-118-11785-9

QuickBooks 2014
For Dummies
978-1-118-72005-9

Small Business Marketing
Kit For Dummies,
3rd Edition
978-1-118-31183-7

Careers

Job Interviews
For Dummies, 4th Edition
978-1-118-11290-8

Job Searching with Social
Media For Dummies,
2nd Edition
978-1-118-67856-5

Personal Branding
For Dummies
978-1-118-11792-7

Resumes For Dummies,
6th Edition
978-0-470-87361-8

Starting an Etsy Business
For Dummies, 2nd Edition
978-1-118-59024-9

Diet & Nutrition

Belly Fat Diet For Dummies
978-1-118-34585-6

Mediterranean Diet
For Dummies
978-1-118-71525-3

Nutrition For Dummies,
5th Edition
978-0-470-93231-5

Digital Photography

Digital SLR Photography
All-in-One For Dummies,
2nd Edition
978-1-118-59082-9

Digital SLR Video &
Filmmaking For Dummies
978-1-118-36598-4

Photoshop Elements 12
For Dummies
978-1-118-72714-0

Gardening

Herb Gardening
For Dummies, 2nd Edition
978-0-470-61778-6

Gardening with Free-Range
Chickens For Dummies
978-1-118-54754-0

Health

Boosting Your Immunity
For Dummies
978-1-118-40200-9

Diabetes For Dummies,
4th Edition
978-1-118-29447-5

Living Paleo For Dummies
978-1-118-29405-5

Big Data

Big Data For Dummies
978-1-118-50422-2

Data Visualization
For Dummies
978-1-118-50289-1

Hadoop For Dummies
978-1-118-60755-8

Language &
Foreign Language

500 Spanish Verbs
For Dummies
978-1-118-02382-2

English Grammar
For Dummies, 2nd Edition
978-0-470-54664-2

French All-in-One
For Dummies
978-1-118-22815-9

German Essentials
For Dummies
978-1-118-18422-6

Italian For Dummies,
2nd Edition
978-1-118-00465-4

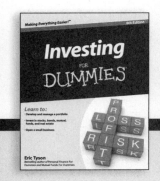 Available in print and e-book formats.

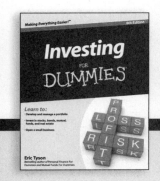
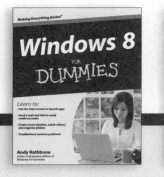

Math & Science

Algebra I For Dummies,
2nd Edition
978-0-470-55964-2

Anatomy and Physiology
For Dummies, 2nd Edition
978-0-470-92326-9

Astronomy For Dummies,
3rd Edition
978-1-118-37697-3

Biology For Dummies,
2nd Edition
978-0-470-59875-7

Chemistry For Dummies,
2nd Edition
978-1-118-00730-3

1001 Algebra II Practice
Problems For Dummies
978-1-118-44662-1

Microsoft Office

Excel 2013 For Dummies
978-1-118-51012-4

Office 2013 All-in-One
For Dummies
978-1-118-51636-2

PowerPoint 2013
For Dummies
978-1-118-50253-2

Word 2013 For Dummies
978-1-118-49123-2

Music

Blues Harmonica
For Dummies
978-1-118-25269-7

Guitar For Dummies,
3rd Edition
978-1-118-11554-1

iPod & iTunes
For Dummies, 10th Edition
978-1-118-50864-0

Programming

Beginning Programming
with C For Dummies
978-1-118-73763-7

Excel VBA Programming
For Dummies, 3rd Edition
978-1-118-49037-2

Java For Dummies,
6th Edition
978-1-118-40780-6

Religion & Inspiration

The Bible For Dummies
978-0-7645-5296-0

Buddhism For Dummies,
2nd Edition
978-1-118-02379-2

Catholicism For Dummies,
2nd Edition
978-1-118-07778-8

Self-Help & Relationships

Beating Sugar Addiction
For Dummies
978-1-118-54645-1

Meditation For Dummies,
3rd Edition
978-1-118-29144-3

Seniors

Laptops For Seniors
For Dummies, 3rd Edition
978-1-118-71105-7

Computers For Seniors
For Dummies, 3rd Edition
978-1-118-11553-4

iPad For Seniors
For Dummies, 6th Edition
978-1-118-72826-0

Social Security
For Dummies
978-1-118-20573-0

Smartphones & Tablets

Android Phones
For Dummies, 2nd Edition
978-1-118-72030-1

Nexus Tablets
For Dummies
978-1-118-77243-0

Samsung Galaxy S 4
For Dummies
978-1-118-64222-1

Samsung Galaxy Tabs
For Dummies
978-1-118-77294-2

Test Prep

ACT For Dummies,
5th Edition
978-1-118-01259-8

ASVAB For Dummies,
3rd Edition
978-0-470-63760-9

GRE For Dummies,
7th Edition
978-0-470-88921-3

Officer Candidate Tests
For Dummies
978-0-470-59876-4

Physician's Assistant Exam
For Dummies
978-1-118-11556-5

Series 7 Exam For Dummie
978-0-470-09932-2

Windows 8

Windows 8.1 All-in-One
For Dummies
978-1-118-82087-2

Windows 8.1 For Dummies
978-1-118-82121-3

Windows 8.1 For Dummies
Book + DVD Bundle
978-1-118-82107-7

e **Available in print and e-book formats.**

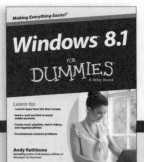

Available wherever books are sold. **For more information or to order direct visit www.dummies.com**

Take Dummies with you everywhere you go!

Whether you are excited about e-books, want more from the web, must have your mobile apps, or are swept up in social media, Dummies makes everything easier.

Leverage the Power

For Dummies is the global leader in the reference category and one of the most trusted and highly regarded brands in the world. No longer just focused on books, customers now have access to the For Dummies content they need in the format they want. Let us help you develop a solution that will fit your brand and help you connect with your customers.

Advertising & Sponsorships

Connect with an engaged audience on a powerful multimedia site, and position your message alongside expert how-to content.

Targeted ads • Video • Email marketing • Microsites • Sweepstakes sponsorship

21 Million Monthly Page Views & 13 Million Unique Visitors